HARCOURT

Math

Problem Solving and Reading Strategies Workbook

TEACHER EDITION

Grade 2

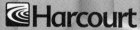

Harcourt

Orlando Austin Chicago New York Toronto London San Diego

Visit *The Learning Site!*
www.harcourtschool.com

REPRODUCING COPIES FOR STUDENTS

This Teacher's Edition contains full-size student pages with answers printed in non-reproducible blue ink.

It may be necessary to adjust the exposure control on your photocopy machine to a lighter setting to ensure that blue answers do not reproduce.

Printed in the United States of America

ISBN 0-15-336531-5

1 2 3 4 5 6 7 8 9 10 054 10 09 08 07 06 05 04 03

CONTENTS

Name ________________________________

Understand Plan Solve Check

Tens

Solve.

1. Meg counted 20 beetles in the woods. How many groups of ten beetles did she count?

   2 groups of ten

2. Maya saw 40 caterpillars on her lawn. How many groups of ten caterpillars did she see?

   4 groups of ten

3. Terry has an ant farm with 100 ants. How many groups of ten ants does he have?

   10 groups of ten

4. Kwan counts 50 fireflies. How many groups of ten fireflies does he count?

   5 groups of ten

5. How many grasshoppers does it take to make 6 groups of ten?

   60 grasshoppers

6. How many honey bees does it take to make 9 groups of ten?

   90 honey bees

Mark the correct answer.

7. Ethan saw 40 butterflies in the garden. How many groups of ten butterflies did he see?

   ○ 2 groups of ten
   ● 4 groups of ten
   ○ 20 groups of ten
   ○ 40 groups of ten

8. Tate has 3 bags of seeds. Each bag has 10 seeds. How many seeds does she have?

   ○ 3 seeds
   ○ 10 seeds
   ○ 15 seeds
   ● 30 seeds

Name ______________________________

Understand Plan Solve Check

Tens and Ones

Check children's drawings.

Draw a model. Then solve.

1. Julie puts her rocks in 1 group of ten. She has 6 rocks left over. How many rocks does she have?

   16 rocks

2. Nick puts his stickers in 6 groups of ten. He has 7 left over. How many stickers does he have?

   67 stickers

3. Josh puts his cars in 3 groups of ten. He has 3 cars left over. How many cars does he have?

   33 cars

Mark the correct answer.

4. Which is the number?

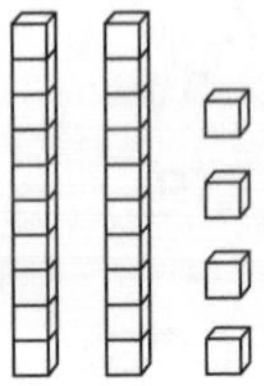

- ○ 20
- ● 24
- ○ 40
- ○ 42

5. Which number is the same as 40 + 9?

- ○ 40
- ○ 44
- ● 49
- ○ 94

Name ____________________

Understand | Plan | Solve | Check

Understand Place Value

Write the value of each digit.

1. Scott sorted his marbles into 5 groups of ten. He had 3 marbles left over. How many marbles did Scott have?

   53 marbles

2. Kari made 3 stacks of blocks. Each stack had 10 blocks. How many blocks did she stack?

   30 blocks

3. Marty had 73 bricks. He put them in stacks of ten. How many bricks did Marty stack?

   70 bricks

4. Sally wrote the number 27 on a piece of paper. What is the value of the digit 2 in the number?

   20

5. Tony saw a number on a sign. The number had 5 ones and 8 tens. What was the number Tony saw?

   85

6. Han thought of a number. She said her number had 2 tens and 3 ones. What was the number?

   23

Mark the correct answer.

7. What is the value of the underlined digit?

   $\underline{3}5$

   - ○ 3
   - ○ 5
   - ● 30
   - ○ 50

8. What is the value of the underlined digit?

   $8\underline{3}$

   - ● 3
   - ○ 8
   - ○ 30
   - ○ 80

Name ____________________

LESSON 1.4

Understand Plan Solve Check

Read and Write Numbers to 100

Write the number three different ways.

1. Mr. Torres has 5 boxes with 10 books in each. He buys 3 more books. How many books does he have in all?

__5__ tens __3__ ones

__50__ + __3__

__53__ books

2. Ms. Francis has 7 boxes with 10 books in each. She buys 6 more. How many books does she have in all?

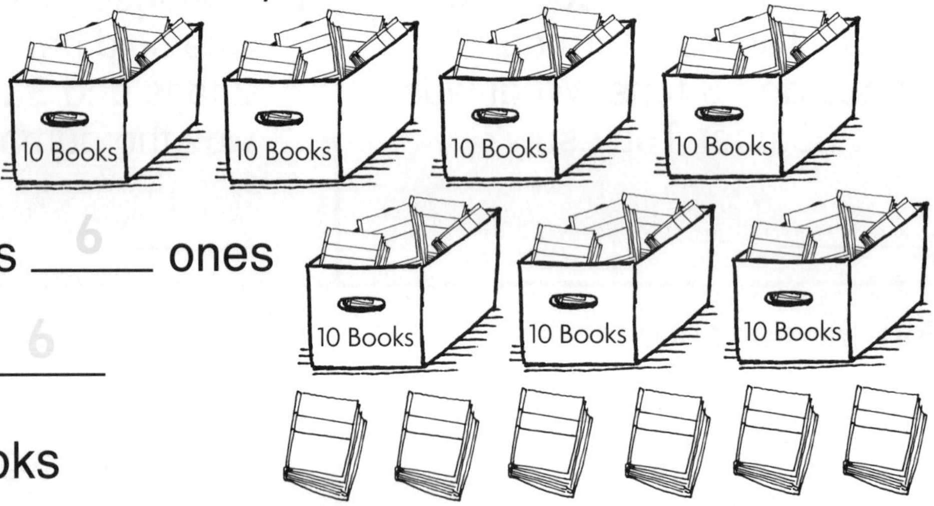

__7__ tens __6__ ones

__70__ + __6__

__76__ books

Mark the correct answer.

3. Which number has 2 tens and 8 ones?

- ○ 73
- ○ 47
- ● 28
- ○ 19

4. Which number is the same as 60 + 7?

- ○ 32
- ● 67
- ○ 77
- ○ 83

Name ______________________________

Understand Plan Solve Check

Algebra: Different Ways to Show Numbers

Solve.
Circle the answer.

1. Pam wrote the number 74 on the board. What is another way she could have written the number?

   7 tens 4 ones   40 + 7

2. Len wrote 2 tens 8 ones on a piece of paper. What is another way Len could have written the number?

   80 + 2   28

3. Lisa used tens and ones to show 36. How did Lisa show the number?

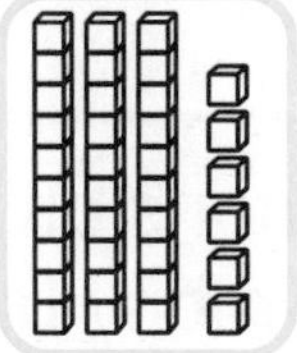
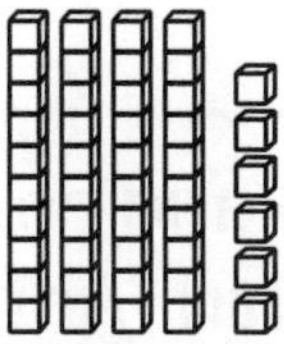

4. Mike drew a picture to show 15. Which picture did Mike draw?

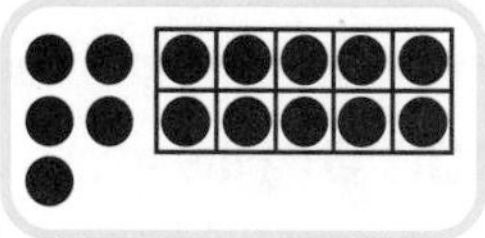
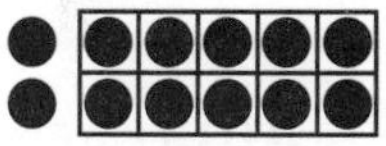

5. José wrote the number 25 in a place value chart. Which chart did he use?

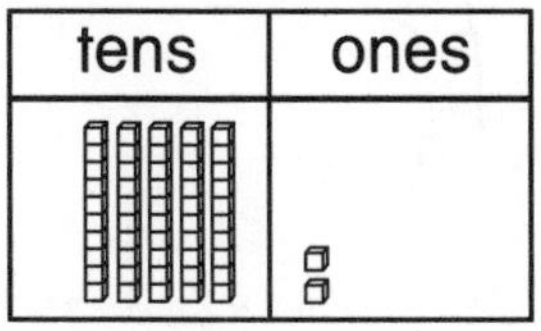

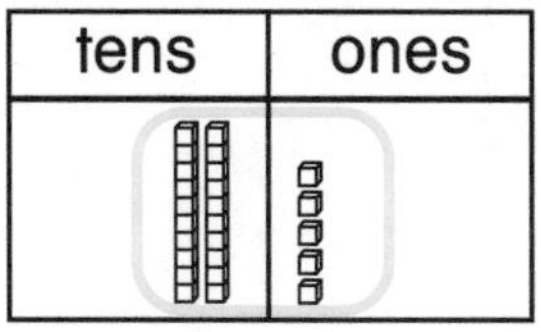

6. Suni wrote 10 + 8 on the board. What is another way she could have shown the number?

   8 tens 1 one

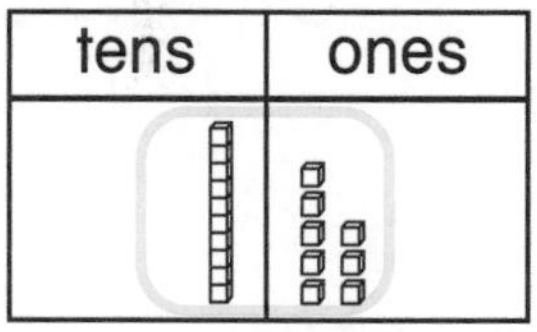

Mark the correct answer.

7. What is another way to show 76?

   ○ 7 + 60
   ○ 6 tens 7 ones
   ○ 70 + 6
   ○ 7 tens 7 ones

8. What is another way to show 41?

   ○ 10 + 4
   ○ 4 tens 1 one
   ○ 4 tens 4 ones
   ○ 40 + 4

Name ______________________________

Understand Plan Solve Check

Reading Strategy • Create Mental Images

Picture the estimates in your mind.
Then circle the most reasonable estimate.

1. James has some cats. About how many cats might he have?

3   30   100

2. Shelby has these pencils in a box. About how many pencils might be in the box?

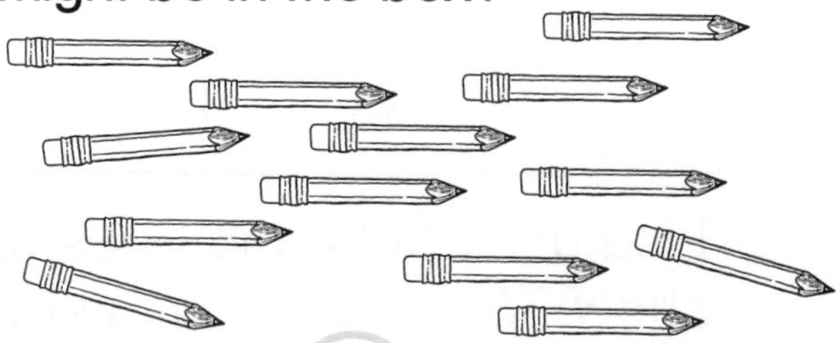

2   20   100

3. Dan gives each of his classmates a card. About how many cards might that be?

3   30   100

4. Maria counts buttons on her shirt. About how many buttons might be on her shirt?

7   50   100

5. Todd fills a large bag with toy rings. About how many rings might be in the bag?

8   20   100

6. Lani returns books to the library. About how many books might she have returned?

6   60   100

Name ____________________

Understand | Plan | Solve | Check

Algebra: Counting on a Number Line

Solve. Use the number line to help you.

1. 50 51 52 53 54 55 56 57 58 59 60 61 62 63 64 65

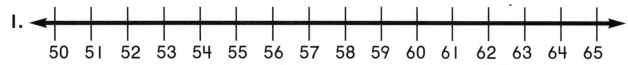

Wasaki started on number 54.
He counted forward 8 jumps.
To what number did he count? 62

---

2. 10 11 12 13 14 15 16 17 18 19 20 21 22 23 24 25

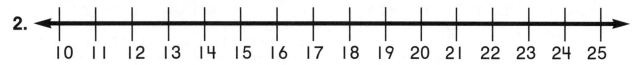

Kaya started on number 17.
She counted backward 5 jumps.
To what number did she count? 12

---

3. 20 21 22 23 24 25 26 27 28 29 30 31 32 33 34 35

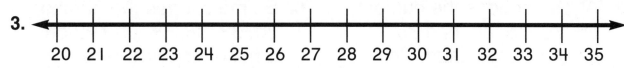

Darnell started on number 32.
He counted backward 6 jumps.
To what number did he count? 26

Use the number line.
Mark the correct answer.

80 81 82 83 84 85 86 87 88 89 90 91 92 93 94 95

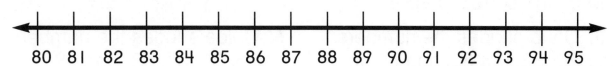

4. Start on 83. Count forward 7. To what number do you count?

○ 89 ● 90

○ 91 ○ 92

5. Start on 92. Count backward 5. To what number do you count?

○ 89 ○ 88

● 87 ○ 86

Understand | Plan | Solve | Check

Algebra: Hundred Chart and Skip-Counting Patterns

Solve. Use the hundred chart to help you.

1	2	3	4	5	6	7	8	9	10
11	12	13	14	15	16	17	18	19	20
21	22	23	24	25	26	27	28	29	30
31	32	33	34	35	36	37	38	39	40
41	42	43	44	45	46	47	48	49	50
51	52	53	54	55	56	57	58	59	60
61	62	63	64	65	66	67	68	69	70
71	72	73	74	75	76	77	78	79	80
81	82	83	84	85	86	87	88	89	90
91	92	93	94	95	96	97	98	99	100

1. Dan shades the numbers 42, 44, 46, 48, and 50 on a hundred chart. By what number is he skip-counting?

   2

2. April shades the numbers 60, 64, 68, 72, and 76 on a hundred chart. By what number is she skip-counting?

   4

3. Alyssa shades the numbers 65, 70, 75, 80, and 85 on a hundred chart. She continues the pattern. What is the next number Alyssa shades?

   90

4. Emma shades the numbers 30, 33, 36, 39, and 42 on a hundred chart. She continues the pattern. What is the next number Emma shades?

   45

Mark the correct answer.

5. Doug shades the numbers 20, 30, 40, 50, and 60 on a hundred chart. By what number is he skip-counting?

   ○ 4　○ 5
   ○ 8　● 10

6. Chloe shades the numbers 25, 31, 37, 43, and 49 on a hundred chart. She continues the pattern. What is the next number Chloe shades?

   ○ 52　○ 53
   ○ 54　● 55

Name ______________________________

LESSON 2.3

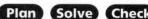

Understand Plan Solve Check

Even and Odd

Solve. Use  to help.
Write **even** or **odd**.

1. Caleb has 8 cubes and Kito has 6 cubes. Do they have an even or an odd number of cubes? even

2. Haley has 15 cubes and Jordan has 21 cubes. Do they have an even or an odd number of cubes? even

3. Asha has 14 cubes and José has 19 cubes. Do they have an even or an odd number of cubes? odd

4. Jina has 8 cubes and Shani has 18 cubes. Do they have an even or an odd number of cubes? even

5. Jiro has 7 cubes and Cole has 10 cubes. Do they have an even or an odd number of cubes? odd

---

Mark the correct answer.

6. Which number is odd?
   - ○ 34
   - ○ 66
   - ○ 48
   - ● 87

7. Which number is even?
   - ○ 27
   - ○ 73
   - ● 56
   - ○ 95

Name ______________________

Understand Plan Solve Check

Reading Strategy: Make Predictions

Sometimes a problem asks you to tell what will happen next.

Mark wants to fill up his photo album. Each page holds 3 pictures. There are 6 pages. How many pictures will Mark use?

Make a chart. Look for a pattern.

number of pages	1	2	3	4	5	6
number of pictures	3	6	9	12	15	18

1. What is the pattern? add 3

2. How many pictures do 6 pages hold? 18

3. Mark will use 18 pictures.

Use the chart to figure out what will happen. Then solve.

4. 4 skateboarders are putting on knee and elbow pads. How many pads will they use in all?

skateboarders	1	2	3	4
number of pads	4	8	12	16

What is the pattern? add 4

How many pads do 4 skateboarders need? 16 pads

The skateboarders will use 16 pads.

Name ______________________________

Understand Plan Solve Check

Ordinal Numbers

Solve.

1. Tami is seventh in line. Mia is just behind her. In what position is Mia?

   eighth or 8th

2. Adam is on the 5th floor. He walks up to the next floor. What floor is he on now?

   sixth or 6th

3. Irene is third in line. Nick is just in front of her. In what position is Nick?

   second or 2nd

4. Avi is 9th in line. Kara is just behind him. In what position is Kara?

   tenth or 10th

5. There are 15 cars in line. A green car is last. A blue car is just in front of the green car. In what position is the blue car?

   fourteenth or 14th

6. Lamar finishes second in a race. He crosses the finish line just behind Kurt. In what position is Kurt?

   first or 1st

Mark the correct answer.

7. I am just after the 12th person in line. What is my position?

   - ○ 10th
   - ● 13th
   - ○ 11th
   - ○ 14th

8. I am just before the eighth person in line. What is my position?

   - ● 7th
   - ○ 10th
   - ○ 9th
   - ○ 12th

Name ______________________________

Understand Plan Solve Check

Algebra: Compare Numbers: >, <, or =

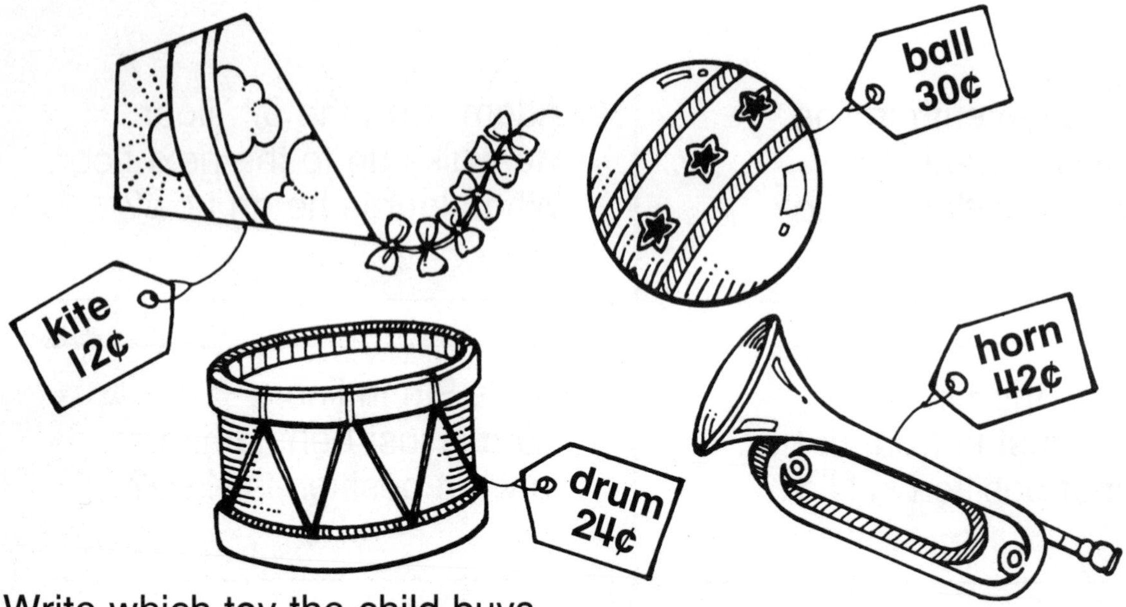

Write which toy the child buys.

1. Tom buys a toy. The price of the toy is greater than 35¢.

   horn

2. Jessie buys a toy. The price of the toy is less than 15¢.

   kite

3. Matt buys a toy. The price of the toy is greater than 25¢ and less than 35¢.

   ball

4. Becky buys a toy. The price of the toy is greater than 20¢ and less than 25¢.

   drum

Mark the correct answer.

5. Choose >, <, or =.

   27 ◯ 19

   ◯ <
   ● >
   ◯ =

6. Choose >, <, or =.

   46 ◯ 64

   ● <
   ◯ >
   ◯ =

Understand Plan Solve Check

Order Numbers to 100

Solve.

1. Mary numbered her problems 10, 11, 13, 14, and 15. What number did she leave out?

   12

2. David is putting number blocks in order. He lines up blocks 31, 32, and 33. What block is next?

   34

3. Joe's house is between two houses numbered 63 and 65. What is the number of Joe's house?

   64

4. There are three lockers. The first one is number 23. The last one is number 25. What is the number of the locker between 23 and 25?

   24

5. Tara likes to count backward. She counts 12, 11, 9, 8. What number did Tara leave out?

   10

6. Jerry is counting down for the race. He counts 5, 4, 3, 1. What number did Jerry leave out?

   2

Mark the correct answer.

7. 15, ______, 17, 18

   ○ 12
   ○ 13
   ○ 14
   ● 16

8. 28, 29, ______, 31

   ○ 26
   ○ 27
   ● 30
   ○ 32

Name ______________________________

Understand Plan Solve Check

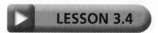

10 More, 10 Less

Solve.

1. Nari counts 12 birds. Josh counts 10 more than Nari. How many birds does Josh count?

   ___22___ birds

2. Rico saved 65¢ Chris saved 10¢ less. How much did Chris save?

   ___55___ ¢

3. Tony swims for 33 minutes. Lita swims 10 minutes longer. How many minutes does Lita swim?

   ___43___ minutes

4. Mark buys 15 marbles. Jack buys 10 fewer marbles. How many marbles does Jack buy?

   ___5___ marbles

5. Kate's class has 29 students. Ruth's class has 10 fewer students. How many students does Ruth's class have?

   ___19___ students

6. Dena has 6 markers. She gets 10 more. How many markers does Dena have now?

   ___16___ markers

Mark the correct answer.

7. What number is 10 more than 53?

   ○ 43

   ○ 52

   ○ 54

   ● 63

8. What number is 10 less than 71?

   ○ 17

   ● 61

   ○ 70

   ○ 81

Name ______________________________ **LESSON 3.5**

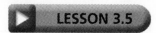

Understand | Plan | Solve | Check

Reading Strategy • Create Mental Images

Jake has 19 books.
About how many books does he have?
Round to the nearest ten.

Picture the problem.

Choose a way to solve the problem. Make a model  .
Draw a picture  .

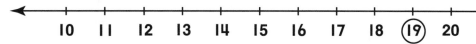

Solve. ← 10 11 12 13 14 15 16 17 18 (19) 20 →

19 is closer to __20__ than to __10__.

Jack has about __20__ books.

Picture the problems.
Then solve.

1. Mai has 32 pennies. Does she have about 30 or about 40 pennies?

32 is closer to __30__

Mai has about __30__ pennies.

2. Del has 48 markers. Does she have about 40 or about 50 markers?

48 is closer to __50__

Del has about __50__ markers.

3. Dan walks 14 blocks. Does he walk about 10 or about 20 blocks?

14 is closer to __10__

Dan walks about __10__ blocks.

4. Ho rides his bicycle for 28 minutes. Does he ride for about 20 or about 30 minutes?

28 is closer to __30__

Ho rides for about __30__ minutes.

Name ______________________________

Understand Plan Solve Check

Take a Survey on a Tally Table

The tally table shows the favorite sports of the children in Mr. Kim's class.

Favorite Sport	
Sport	**Tally**
Swimming	卌 II
Biking	卌 卌
Rollerblading	IIII
Running	III

Use the table to solve.

1. How many children like rollerblading best?

4 children

2. Which sport do 7 children like best?

swimming

3. Which sport do the most children like best?

biking

4. Which sport do the fewest children like best?

running

5. How many more children chose biking than swimming?

3 children

6. How many more children chose swimming than running?

4 children

Mark the correct answer.

7. How many fewer children chose rollerblading than biking?

- ● 6
- ○ 4
- ○ 5
- ○ 3

8. How many fewer children chose swimming than biking?

- ○ 6
- ○ 4
- ○ 5
- ● 3

Name ______________________________

Understand Plan Solve Check

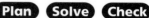

Use Data in Tables

Jan took a survey. She asked children in her group to name their favorite season. Then she asked her whole class the same question.

Favorite Season for Jan's Group

Season	Tally
Winter	||
Spring	|
Summer	𝍸
Fall	|

Favorite Season for Jan's Class

Season	Tally
Winter	|||
Spring	||||
Summer	𝍸 𝍸 ||||
Fall	||

Use the tally tables to solve.

1. How many children in Jan's group like spring best?

   1 ______________________

2. How many children in Jan's class like winter best?

   3 ______________________

3. How many children in the group like fall or winter best?

   3 ______________________

4. How many children in the class like spring or summer best?

   18 ______________________

Mark the correct answer.

5. Which season is the favorite in Jan's class?

   ○ winter ○ spring
   ● summer ○ fall

6. Which season is the favorite of 2 children in the group?

   ● winter ○ spring
   ○ summer ○ fall

Name ______________________________

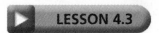

Understand Plan Solve Check

Make a Concrete Graph

The children in Mr. Bozak's class collected leaves. They made a concrete graph to show what trees the leaves came from.

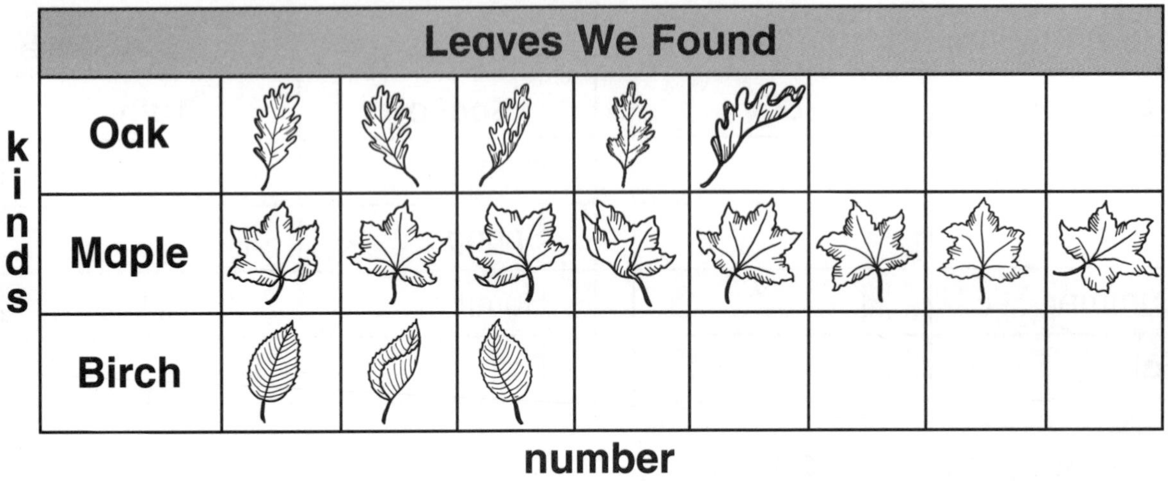

Use the graph to solve.

1. How many oak leaves did the class find?

   ___5___ oak leaves

2. How many maple leaves did the class find?

   ___8___ maple leaves

3. Did the class find more oak leaves or more birch leaves?

   ___oak___ leaves

4. Did the class find more birch leaves or more maple leaves?

   ___maple___ leaves

Mark the correct answer.

5. How many leaves did the class find that were not oak leaves?

   ○ 8 ● 11
   ○ 13 ○ 16

6. How many leaves did the class find in all?

   ○ 8 ○ 11
   ○ 13 ● 16

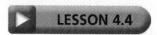

Understand Plan Solve Check

Make a Pictograph

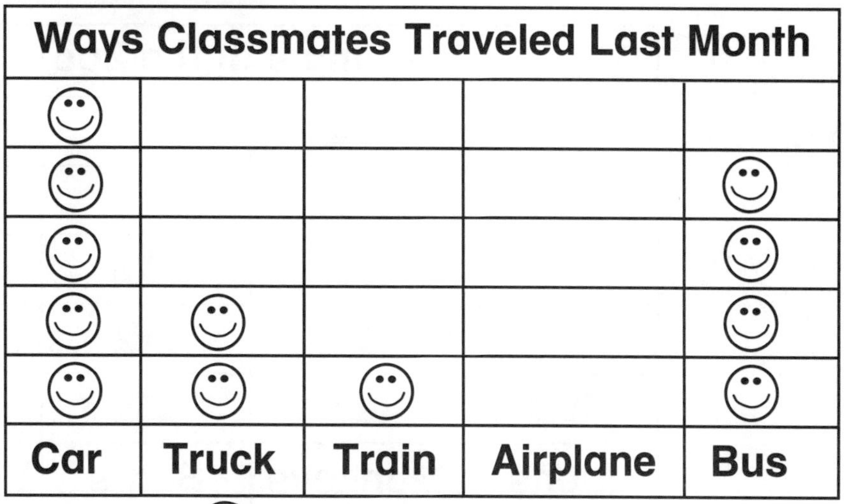

Key: Each ☺ stands for 5 children.

Use the graph to solve.

1. How many classmates rode in a truck last month?

   ____10____

2. How many classmates rode in an airplane?

   ____0____

3. What did 20 classmates travel in last month?

   ____bus____

4. How many more classmates rode in a truck than in a train?

   ____5____

Solve. Use the graph. Mark the best answer.

5. In what did the most classmates travel last month?

   ○ bus ○ train
   ● car ○ truck

6. In what did the fewest classmates travel last month?

   ● airplane ○ train
   ○ car ○ truck

Name ________________________________

Understand Plan Solve Check

Reading Strategy • Use Graphic Aids

Chen saw this graph in a book. He used the graph to answer a question.

If the zoo gets two more lions, how many lions will it have?

4 lions

Animals at the Zoo			
	ZOO		
	ZOO		
	ZOO	ZOO	
	ZOO	ZOO	ZOO
ZOO	ZOO	ZOO	ZOO
Lions	**Monkeys**	**Bears**	**Elephants**

Key: Each ZOO stands for 2 animals.

Use the graph to solve.

1. How many animals does each ZOO stand for?

   2 animals

2. How many animals does the graph show in all?

   22 animals

3. Of which animal does the zoo have the least?

   lions

4. Of which animal does the zoo have the most?

   monkeys

5. The zoo wants to get two more elephants. How many elephants will it have then?

   6 elephants

6. The zoo is going to give 4 monkeys to another zoo. How many monkeys will it have left?

   6 monkeys

Name ______________________

Understand Plan Solve Check

Count On

Count on to find the sum.

1. There are 6 kites in the air. There are 2 kites on the ground. How many kites are there?

   6 + 2 = __8__ kites

2. Joyce had 5 crayons. Larry gave her 1 crayon. How many crayons does Joyce have now?

   5 + 1 = __6__ crayons

3. Gary drew 4 pictures. Then he drew 2 more. How many pictures did Gary draw?

   4 + 2 = __6__ pictures

4. There are 9 girls. There are 3 boys. How many children are there?

   9 + 3 = __12__ children

Mark the correct answer.

5. Bella has 7 red pencils and 2 white pencils. How many pencils does Bella have?

   ○ 7
   ● 9
   ○ 10
   ○ 11

6. There are 10 small cats and 2 large cats. How many cats are there?

   ○ 2
   ○ 8
   ○ 10
   ● 12

Name ______________________

Understand Plan Solve Check

Doubles and Doubles Plus One

Draw a picture.
Solve.

Check children's drawings.

1. Sue has 6 green apples and 7 red apples. How many apples does she have? 13 apples	
2. Ian has 3 dimes. Erika has 1 more dime than Ian. How many dimes do they have together? 7 dimes	
3. 5 people ride in a red car and 5 people ride in a green car. How many people ride in all? 10 people	
4. Amy collects 8 shells. Then she collects 9 more. How many shells does she collect? 17 shells	

Mark the correct answer.

5. Which is 1 more than 7 + 7?
   - ○ 7 + 6
   - ● 7 + 8
   - ○ 8 + 8
   - ○ 8 + 9

6. Which is 1 less than 6 + 6?
   - ○ 7 + 7
   - ○ 6 + 7
   - ● 6 + 5
   - ○ 5 + 5

Name ______________________________

Make a Ten

Understand Plan Solve Check

Check children's drawings.

Draw ◯. Make a ten. Write the sum.

1. Mr. Long bought 8 red apples and 5 green apples. How many apples did he buy?

13 apples

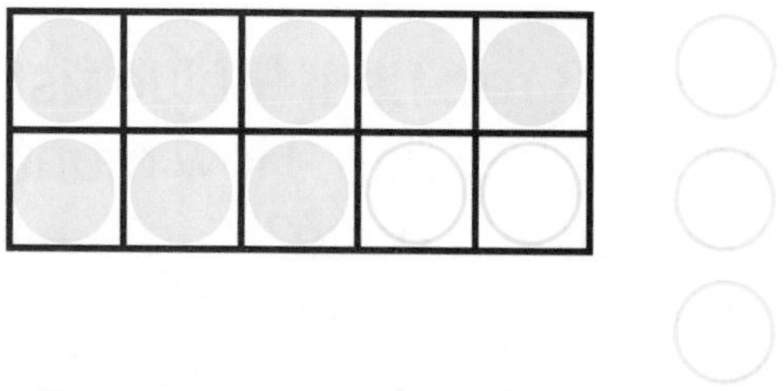

2. Ted sees 6 red hens and 9 white hens. How many hens does he see?

15 hens

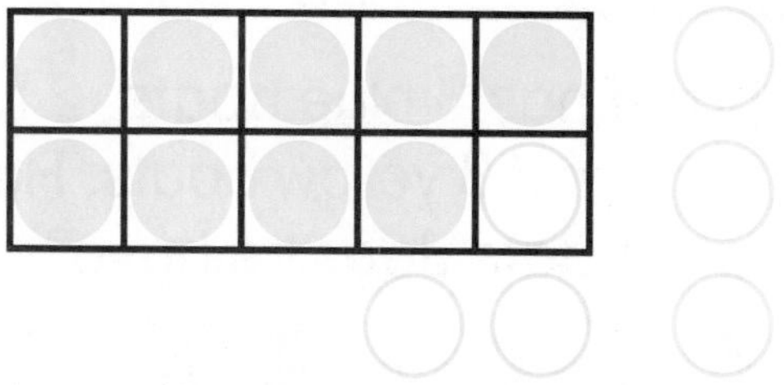

3. Julie has 9 toy horses. She gets 4 more. How many horses does Julie have?

13 horses

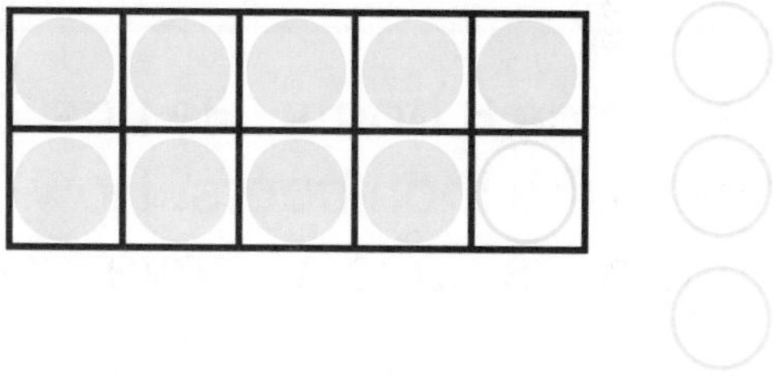

4. Ryan has 4 dogs and 7 cats. How many pets does Ryan have?

11 pets

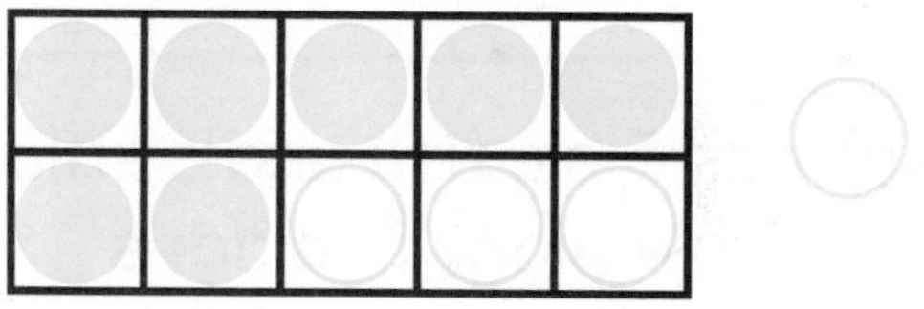

Mark the correct answer.

5. Jo has 7 dolls. Su has 6 more dolls than Jo. How many dolls does Su have?

- ◯ 15
- ◯ 14
- ● 13
- ◯ 12

6. Lang read 8 books. Ken read 6 more books than Larry. How many books did Ken read?

- ● 14
- ◯ 15
- ◯ 16
- ◯ 17

Name ______________________________

Understand Plan Solve Check

Algebra: Add 3 Numbers

Draw a picture. Then write the number sentence.

1. Lin has 3 red fish, 4 blue fish, and 5 yellow fish. How many fish does Lin have?

   3 + 4 + 5 = 12 fish

2. Charlie has 3 blue boats, 2 red boats, and 3 yellow boats. How many boats does he have?

   3 + 2 + 3 = 8 boats

3. Jason has 8 boats. He has 9 more rafts than boats. How many rafts does he have?

   8 + 9 = 17 rafts

4. Kali has 5 big fish and 6 little fish. How many fish does she have?

   5 + 6 = 11 fish

Mark the correct answer.

5. Ron has 1 red car, 4 green cars, and 5 blue cars. How many cars does he have?

   ○ 9 ○ 11
   ● 10 ○ 12

6. Lisa sees 2 white birds, 4 black birds, and 3 brown birds. How many birds does she see?

   ○ 6 ○ 8
   ○ 7 ● 9

Name ____________________

Understand Plan Solve Check

Reading Strategy • Use Picture Clues

Using picture clues can help you solve problems.

Read the problem. Use picture clues to help you solve it.

There are 3 crabs in the water.

There are 3 crabs in the sand.

There are 2 crabs on a rock.

How many crabs are there in all? 8 crabs

Look for picture clues. Solve the problems.

1. Jake saw 3 turtles at the beach. He saw 2 starfish. He saw 2 seagulls. How many animals did Jake see in all?

   7 animals

---

2. Ruby found 4 shells. Sara found 3 shells. Molly found 2 shells. How many shells did they find in all?

   9 shells

Name ____

Understand Plan Solve Check

Count Back

Write the number sentence.

1. Raj had 8 carrot sticks. He ate 2 of them. How many carrot sticks did Raj have left?

   8 − 2 = 6 carrot sticks

2. Nina had 10 golf balls. She lost 1 of them. How many golf balls did Nina have left?

   10 − 1 = 9 golf balls

3. Ivan and Kim made a tower with 11 blocks. The top 3 blocks fell off. How many blocks were left in the tower?

   11 − 3 = 8 blocks

4. Tina has 9 bags of popcorn. There are 3 large bags. The rest are small bags. How many small bags does Tina have?

   9 − 3 = 6 small bags

5. The rose bush has 6 flowers. Alana picks 2 of them. How many roses are left on the bush?

   6 − 2 = 4 roses

6. There are 7 kittens playing. Then 3 of them run to their mother. How many kittens are still playing?

   7 − 3 = 4 kittens

Mark the correct answer.

7. Roy had 10 toy cars. He gave away 3. How many toy cars did he have left?

   ○ 3 ● 7
   ○ 4 ○ 8

8. There are 12 birds on the roof. Then 2 of them fly away. How many birds are left?

   ○ 9 ○ 11
   ● 10 ○ 12

Name ____________________

Understand Plan Solve Check

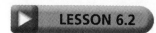

Algebra: Fact Families

Write the fact family for the set of numbers.

1. Martha pulls 15 cubes out of a bag.
   7 cubes are red and 8 cubes are blue.

   7 + 8 = 15   8 + 7 = 15

   15 − 7 = 8   15 − 8 = 7

2. Ann Lee pulls 11 cubes out of a bag.
   5 cubes are yellow and 6 cubes are green.

   5 + 6 = 11   6 + 5 = 11

   11 − 5 = 6   11 − 6 = 5

3. Carol pulls 17 cubes out of a bag.
   9 cubes are blue and 8 cubes are red.

   9 + 8 = 17   8 + 9 = 17

   17 − 9 = 8   17 − 8 = 9

Mark the correct answer.

4. Lin has 9 pennies. Leslie gives her 4 more. How many pennies does Lin have?

   ○ 5
   ○ 7
   ● 13
   ○ 14

5. Which belongs in the fact family for the set of numbers?

4	5	9

   ● 9 − 4 = 5
   ○ 5 + 9 = 14
   ○ 14 − 5 = 9
   ○ 5 − 4 = 1

Name ______________________________

Understand Plan Solve Check

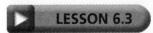

Relate Addition to Subtraction

Solve.

1. There are 7 flowers in Conor's garden. He plants 4 more. How many flowers does Conor have now?

   7 + 4 = 11 flowers

2. Becky has 11 cherries. She eats 4 of them. How many cherries does Becky have left?

   11 − 4 = 7 cherries

3. Tomi bakes 8 pies. Then he bakes 5 more pies. How many pies does Tomi have in all?

   8 + 5 = 13 pies

4. Lea gets 13 flags. She gives 5 flags away. How many flags does Lea still have?

   13 − 5 = 8 flags

5. There are 6 people in the room. Then 4 more people come in. How many people are in the room now?

   6 + 4 = 10 people

6. There are 10 birds in the tree. Then 4 birds fly away. How many birds are in the tree now?

   10 − 4 = 6 birds

Mark the correct answer.

7. Alana has 6 apples. She picks 5 more apples. How many apples does Alana have now?

   ○ 5 ○ 10
   ○ 6 ● 11

8. Greg has 11 apples. He uses 5 apples to make applesauce. How many apples are left?

   ○ 5 ○ 11
   ● 6 ○ 16

Name ____________________

Understand Plan Solve Check

Algebra: Missing Addends

Write the missing addend.

1. Jen has 7 pennies. She finds some more pennies. Now she has 12 pennies. How many pennies did Jen find?

   7 + 5 = 12

   Jen found 5 pennies.

2. Isha drew some pictures yesterday. Today she drew 8 more. Now she has 11 pictures. How many pictures did Isha draw yesterday?

   8 + 3 = 11

   Isha drew 3 pictures yesterday.

3. Max saw 9 green fish and some red fish. He saw 14 fish in all. How many red fish did Max see?

   9 + 5 = 14

   Max saw 5 red fish.

4. Zach has 6 marbles. He finds some more marbles. Now he has 15 marbles. How many marbles did Zach find?

   6 + 9 = 15

   Zach found 9 marbles.

Mark the correct answer.

5. Elly has 7 big boxes and some small boxes. She has 10 boxes in all. How many small boxes does she have?

   ● 3 ○ 7
   ○ 4 ○ 10

6. There are 13 cows in a field. There are 4 white cows. The rest are brown. How many brown cows are there?

   ○ 7 ○ 10
   ● 9 ○ 13

Name ____________________

Understand Plan Solve Check

Algebra: Names for Numbers

Solve.

1. Miko wrote a number name for 14. Her number name used addition. It used the number 7. What was Miko's number name for 14?

   7 + 7

2. Alvin wrote a number name for 6. His number name used subtraction. It began with the number 10. What was Alvin's number name for 6?

   10 − 4

3. Umi wrote a number name for 5. Her number name used subtraction. It began with the number 8. What was Umi's number name for 5?

   8 − 3

4. Craig wrote a number name for 18. His number name used addition. It used the number 9. What was Craig's number name for 18?

   9 + 9

5. Molly wrote a number name for 12. Her number name used addition. It used the number 7. What was Molly's number name for 12?

   7 + 5

6. Raul wrote a number name for 7. His number name used subtraction. It began with the number 15. What was Raul's number name for 7?

   15 − 8

Mark the correct answer.

7. Which is a number name for 9?

   ○ 3 + 5 ● 11 − 2

   ○ 6 + 4 ○ 15 − 0

8. Which is a number name for 12?

   ○ 15 − 5 ○ 6 + 5

   ● 15 − 3 ○ 7 + 6

Name ______________________________

Understand Plan Solve Check

Reading Strategy • Create Mental Images

Think about what is happening in the problem.
Then draw a picture or make a model.
Write the number sentence to solve.

Check children's work.

1. Karla had 3 mice. Then she bought 6 more mice. How many mice did she have?

3 (+) 6 = 9 mice

2. There were 10 cats in the yard. Then 4 of them went into the house. How many cats were still in the yard?

10 (−) 4 = 6 cats

3. Hal saw 6 birds in a tree and 5 birds on the ground. How many birds did Hal see?

6 (+) 5 = 11 birds

4. Jan has 7 goldfish. Ping has 3 goldfish. How many more goldfish does Jan have than Ping?

7 (−) 3 = 4 goldfish

Name ____________________

Understand Plan Solve Check

Mental Math: Add Tens

Solve.
Do your work in the box.

1. Emma read 20 books. Dylan read 40. How many books did they read in all? 60 books	
2. There are 30 children in Class 2A. There are 30 children in Class 2B. How many children are there in all? 60 children	
3. Elisha scored 10 points in Monday's game. She scored 20 points in Wednesday's game. How many points did she score in all? 30 more points	

Mark the correct answer.

4. Which is another way to write 3 tens + 2 tens = 5 tens?

- ○ 20 + 20 = 40
- ● 30 + 20 = 50
- ○ 30 + 40 = 70
- ○ 30 + 50 = 80

5. Which is another way to write 50 + 20 = 70?

- ● 5 tens + 2 tens = 7 tens
- ○ 2 tens + 6 tens = 8 tens
- ○ 4 tens + 5 tens = 9 tens
- ○ 7 tens + 2 tens = 9 tens

Name ______________________

Understand Plan Solve Check

Mental Math: Count On Tens and Ones

Solve.
Count on to add.

Check children's work.

1. There are 63 paper clips on the table. Ms. Kenner puts 20 more on the table. How many paper clips are there in all? 83 paper clips	Say. 63 Count on. 73, 83 $63 + 20 = 83$
2. Nadine has 31 buttons. Her mother gives her 2 more. How many buttons does Nadine have in all? 33 buttons	Say. 31 Count on. 32, 33 $31 + 2 = 33$
3. Herbie has 54 shells. He buys 30 more. How many shells does he have in all? 84 shells	Say. 54 Count on. 64, 74, 84 $54 + 30 = 84$

Mark the correct answer.

4. Which is the sum?
$19 + 3 = \underline{?}$

- ○ 9
- ○ 11
- ● 22
- ○ 27

5. Which is the sum?
$49 + 10 = \underline{?}$

- ○ 39
- ○ 50
- ● 59
- ○ 69

Name ____________________

Understand Plan Solve Check

Regroup Ones as Tens

Use Workmat 3 and 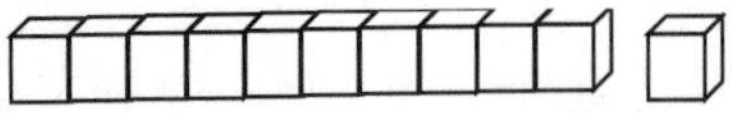 .

Solve.

1. Ben and his father made 12 plain muffins and 8 raisin muffins. How many muffins did they make?

20 muffins

2. It took 15 minutes to make lemonade. It took 7 minutes to clean up. How many minutes did it take in all?

22 minutes

3. Mrs. Lewis used 18 apples for applesauce. Then she used 6 apples to make more applesauce. How many apples did she use?

24 apples

4. The baker made 23 loaves of white bread and 6 loaves of wheat bread. How many loaves of bread did he make?

29 loaves of bread

Mark the correct answer.

5. Maria bought 13 bagels. Then she bought 8 more. How many bagels did she buy?

- ○ 5
- ○ 11
- ○ 15
- ● 21

6. Tasha ate 11 grapes. Then she ate 5 more. How many grapes did Tasha eat?

- ○ 6
- ○ 12
- ● 16
- ○ 26

Name ______________________

Understand Plan Solve Check

Model 2-Digit Addition

Use Workmat 3 and 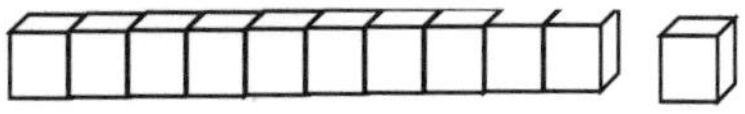 .

Solve.

1. Paul sees 11 deer on Monday. He sees 16 deer on Tuesday. How many deer does he see on both days together?

   27 deer

2. Carol sees 16 rabbits on Tuesday. She sees 21 rabbits on Wednesday. How many rabbits does she see on both days together?

   37 rabbits

3. John sees 15 newts on Wednesday. He sees 9 newts on Thursday. How many newts does he see in all?

   24 newts

4. Natalie sees 12 chipmunks on Thursday. She sees 19 chipmunks on Friday. How many chipmunks does she see on both days together?

   31 chipmunks

Mark the correct answer.

5. Jen sees 13 squirrels on Saturday and 18 squirrels on Sunday. How many squirrels does she see in all?

   ○ 21
   ○ 25
   ● 31
   ○ 35

6. Jon sees 11 spiders on Monday and 12 spiders on Tuesday. How many spiders does he see in all?

   ● 23
   ○ 24
   ○ 29
   ○ 32

Name ______________________________

Understand Plan **Solve** Check

Reading Strategy • Create Mental Images

Ray counts 12 robins and 9 sparrows.
How many birds does he count in all?

Picture the problem.

Choose a way to solve the problem.

Make a model.
Draw a picture.
Write a number sentence.

Solve. 12 + 9 = 21

Ray counts 21 birds.

Picture the problems.
Then solve.

1. Tony has 16 peaches. Amber has 8 peaches. How many peaches do they have in all?

   24 peaches

2. Kira found 34 shells at the beach. Sean found 19 shells. How many shells did they find in all?

   53 shells

3. Loni ran 12 blocks on Monday. He ran 15 blocks on Tuesday. How many blocks did he run altogether?

   27 blocks

4. Tina has 18 flower stickers. She has 24 animal stickers. How many stickers does she have in all?

   42 stickers

Name ______________________

LESSON 8.1

Understand · Plan · Solve · Check

Add 1-Digit Numbers

Use Workmat 3 and base-ten blocks. Add.

1. Ian has 29 animal stickers. He has 5 flower stickers. How many stickers does he have in all?

   34 stickers

2. There are 14 girls and 9 boys in Jani's class. How many children are in Jani's class altogether?

   23 children

3. Kata reads 33 pages of her book in the morning. She reads 6 more pages in the afternoon. How many pages does Kata read in all?

   39 pages

4. Dale makes a necklace with 48 small beads and 8 large beads. How many beads did Dale use to make the necklace?

   56 beads

5. Miko's garden has 56 yellow tulips and 7 red tulips. How many red and yellow tulips are in Miko's garden?

   63 tulips

6. The Rangers won the game against the Eagles. The score was 23 to 8. How many points did both teams score in all?

   31 points

Mark the correct answer.

7. Caleb has 58 stamps in his collection. His grandmother gives him 4 more stamps. How many stamps does Caleb have now?

   ○ 54 ● 62
   ○ 60 ○ 68

8. Sara counts 23 robins in the tree. She counts 7 sparrows in the same tree. How many robins and sparrows did Sara count?

   ○ 16 ○ 33
   ● 30 ○ 40

Name ______________________________

LESSON 8.2

Understand Plan Solve Check

Add 2-Digit Numbers

Use Workmat 3 and [tens and ones blocks]. Add.

1. Jen has 1 ten and 6 ones on her workmat. Then she puts down 2 more tens and 6 more ones. After she regroups, how many ones does Jen have?

   __2__ ones

2. Ollie has 3 tens and 4 ones on his workmat. Then he puts down 1 more ten and 6 more ones. After he regroups, how many tens does Ollie have?

   __5__ tens

3. Yan rides her bicycle 14 blocks to her friend's house. Then she rides 16 blocks to her grandmother's house. How many blocks did Yan ride her bicycle in all?

   __30__ blocks

4. Will does 26 situps in the morning. He does 18 more situps in the evening. How many situps does Will do in all?

   __44__ situps

5. Ida has 24 CDs. Her sister has 36 CDs. How many CDs do Ida and her sister have together?

   __60__ CDs

6. Taylor puts 47 pennies in his piggy bank. He adds 28 more pennies. How many pennies are in Taylor's piggy bank now?

   __75__ pennies

Mark the correct answer.

7. Kyle has 54 marbles. He buys 16 more marbles. How many marbles does Kyle have now?

   ○ 60 ● 70
   ○ 69 ○ 80

8. Debra reads for 36 minutes on Monday. She reads for 28 minutes on Tuesday. How many minutes does Debra read in all?

   ○ 54 ○ 74
   ● 64 ○ 84

Name ______________________________

Understand Plan Solve Check

More 2-Digit Addition

Add. Regroup if you need to.

1. The Mustangs baseball team won 17 games. They lost 14 games. How many games did the Mustangs play?

   31 games

2. The store has 25 large baskets of fruit. It has 15 small baskets of fruit. How many baskets of fruit does the store have in all?

   40 baskets

3. Mark's dog weighs 47 pounds. His cat weighs 16 pounds. How many pounds do the dog and cat weigh together?

   63 pounds

4. Chris swims for 24 minutes. He rides his bike for 48 minutes. How many minutes does Mark swim and ride his bike?

   72 minutes

5. Rita reads 23 pages in her book in the morning. She reads 27 more pages before bed time. How many pages does she read in all?

   50 pages

6. There are 17 houses on one side of Elm Street. There are 16 houses on the other side. How many houses in all are on Elm Street?

   33 houses

Mark the correct answer.

7. The bus travels 34 miles. Then it travels 18 miles. How many miles does the bus travel in all?

   ○ 44 ○ 50
   ○ 46 ● 52

8. Marco buys 2 bags of carrots. One bag has 17 carrots. The other bag has 24 carrots. How many carrots did Marco buy in all?

   ○ 31 ● 41
   ○ 40 ○ 51

Name ______________________

Understand Plan Solve Check

Practice 2-Digit Addition

	Girls	Boys
Grade 2	35	45
Grade 3	41	28

Use the chart to answer the questions.

1. How many children are in Grade 2?

80 children

2. How many boys are there in the two grades?

73 boys

3. How many girls are there in the two grades?

76 girls

4. How many children are in Grade 3?

69 children

Mark the correct answer.

5. There are 26 girls and 29 boys in Grade 5. How many children are there in all?

- ○ 45
- ● 55
- ○ 65

6. There are 36 boys and 40 girls in Grade 1. How many children are there in Grade 1?

- ○ 40
- ○ 64
- ● 76

Name ______________________

Understand Plan Solve Check

Rewrite 2-Digit Addition

Rewrite the numbers.
Solve.

Check children's work.

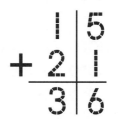

1. There are 15 children on the bus. There are 21 adults on the bus. How many people are on the bus in all? 15 + 21 = 36 people	$\begin{array}{r} 15 \\ +\ 21 \\ \hline 36 \end{array}$
2. Josh and Hanna made a tower with 24 blocks. They added 37 more blocks. How many blocks did Josh and Hanna use in all? 24 + 37 = 61 blocks	+
3. Kendra took the elevator up 18 floors. Then she walked up 7 more floors. How many floors did Kendra go up? 18 + 7 = 25 floors	+
4. Last year the Panthers hit 58 home runs. This year they hit 34 home runs. How many home runs did they hit altogether? 58 + 34 = 92 home runs	+

Mark the correct answer.

5. 49 + 15 =

- ○ 54
- ○ 63
- ○ 55
- ● 64

6. 37 + 16 =

- ○ 43
- ○ 63
- ● 53
- ○ 65

Name ____________________

Understand | Plan | Solve | Check

Estimate Sums

Use the number line to help you round.
Estimate the sum.

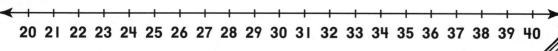

20 21 22 23 24 25 26 27 28 29 30 31 32 33 34 35 36 37 38 39 40

1. There are 22 roses on one bush. There are 31 roses on another bush. About how many roses are there in all? about 50 roses	Check children's work.
2. There are 39 ladybugs on the flowers. There are 23 ladybugs on the tree. About how many ladybugs are there in all? about 60 ladybugs	
3. Pablo found 29 large shells at the beach. He found 24 small shells. About how many shells did Pablo find? about 50 shells	
4. Tami sells 32 bags of peanuts. Her sister sells 38 bags. About how many bags of peanuts did they sell in all? about 70 bags of peanuts	

Estimate the sum.
Mark the correct answer.

5. 39 + 39 =

- ○ 40
- ○ 60
- ○ 50
- ● 80

6. 27 + 24 =

- ● 50
- ○ 80
- ○ 60
- ○ 90

Name ________________________________

Understand Plan Solve Check

Reading Strategy • Choose Important Words

Ray put 25 stickers in one book.
He put 36 stickers in another book.
How many stickers did Ray use in all?

Underline the words that help you solve the problem.

Then solve. 36 + 25 = 61 stickers

Underline the words that help you solve the problem. Then solve.

Check children's work.

1. Haley saw 32 birds this week. She saw 41 birds last week. How many birds did Haley see in all?

   73 birds

2. Fred sees 28 trucks on the highway. He also sees 16 vans. How many trucks and vans does Fred see altogether?

   44 trucks and vans

3. Ella buys two bags of apples. One bag has 12 apples. The other bag has 18 apples. How many apples did Ella buy in all?

   30 apples

Name ______________________________

LESSON 9.1

Understand Plan Solve Check

Mental Math: Subtract Tens

There are 10 trading cards in 1 pack.
Write a subtraction sentence for each problem.

1. Mara has 7 packs of trading cards. She gives Greg 2 of them. How many trading cards does Mara have left?

   7 tens − 2 tens = 5 tens

2. Leon has 8 packs of trading cards. Evan borrows 5 packs. How many trading cards does Leon have left?

   80 − 50 = 30

3. Trudy has 3 packs of trading cards. She gives Philip 1 pack. How many trading cards does Trudy have left?

   30 − 10 = 20

4. Michael has 5 packs of trading cards. Will borrows 4 packs. How many trading cards does Michael have left?

   5 tens − 4 tens = 1 ten

Mark the correct answer.

5. Which is the difference?
   9 tens − 7 tens = ?
   - 2 tens
   - 3 tens
   - 4 tens
   - 8 tens

6. Which is the difference?
   60 − 10 = ?
   - 70
   - 50
   - 30
   - 20

Name ____________________

Understand Plan Solve Check

Mental Math: Count Back Tens and Ones

Write the subtraction sentence. Count back to solve.

1. Matteo made a tower with 62 blocks. His brother took 3 blocks from the top. How many blocks are part of the tower now?

   62 − 3 = 59 blocks

2. Reese played 17 games of tic-tac-toe. She lost only 2 of them. How many games did she win?

   17 − 2 = 15 games

3. Gavin had 87 trading cards. He gave 20 of them away. How many trading cards did he have left?

   87 − 20 = 67 trading cards

4. Ella picked 46 flowers. She gave 10 of them to her grandmother. How many flowers did Ella keep?

   46 − 10 = 36 flowers

5. Hoy bought 20 balloons. On his way to the party, 3 of them popped. How many balloons did he have left?

   20 − 3 = 17 balloons

6. A farmer brought 64 baskets of tomatoes to the market. He sold 30 of them. How many baskets of tomatoes were left?

   64 − 30 = 34 baskets

Mark the correct answer.

7. Tyra brought 54 marbles to her friend's house. She left 3 of them there. How many marbles did she bring home?

   ○ 3 ● 51
   ○ 50 ○ 57

8. Kai bought 25 yo-yos for his party. He gave away 20 to his friends. How many were left?

   ● 5 ○ 20
   ○ 15 ○ 25

Name ______________________________

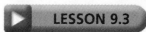

Understand Plan Solve Check

Regroup Tens as Ones

Use Workmat 3 and 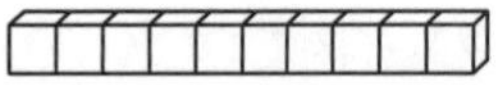 .
Subtract. Write how many tens and ones are left.

1. There are 17 people sledding. Then 9 people go home. How many are left?

   8 people

   0 tens 8 ones

2. There are 23 people sledding. There are 5 people skating. How many more people are sledding than skating?

   18 more people

   1 ten 8 ones

3. There are 22 boys skating. There are 7 girls skating. How many more boys than girls are skating?

   15 more boys

   1 ten 5 ones

4. There are 30 people making snow forts. Then 8 go home. How many people are left?

   22 people

   2 tens 2 ones

Mark the correct answer.

5. There are 38 children at the game. Then 6 go home. How many children are left?

   ○ 22 ● 32
   ○ 26 ○ 44

6. There are 24 red balloons. There are 8 blue balloons. How many more red than blue balloons are there?

   ○ 32 ○ 22
   ○ 26 ● 16

Name ______________________________

LESSON 9.4

Understand **Plan** **Solve** **Check**

Model 2-Digit Subtraction

Use Workmat 3 and 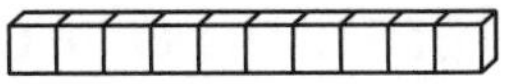 .
Subtract.

1. There are 24 children in a play. 11 children dance. The other children sing. How many children sing?

 13 children

2. There are 30 chairs at the play. There are 13 couches. How many more chairs than couches are there?

 17 more chairs

3. Hannah sold 21 tickets for the play. Anna sold 15 tickets. How many more tickets did Hannah sell than Anna?

 6 more tickets

4. On Friday, 44 people came to the play. On Saturday, 25 fewer people came. How many came on Saturday?

 19 people

Mark the correct answer.

5. There are 25 girls and 16 boys in the play. How many more girls than boys are in the play?

 ● 9
 ○ 14
 ○ 26
 ○ 34

6. Yolanda sold 39 adult tickets and 18 student tickets. How many more adult tickets than student tickets did she sell?

 ○ 11
 ○ 18
 ● 21
 ○ 26

Name ____________________

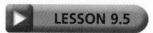

Understand Plan Solve Check

Reading Strategy • Choose Important Words

Important words can help you understand a problem.

Aram has 20 **stamps**.
He uses 4 of them.
How many stamps are **left**?

What is the problem about? stamps

What are you asked to find? How many stamps are left.

Will you add or subtract? subtract

Solve the problem. 20 − 4 = 16

Aram has 16 stamps left.

Solve. Underline important words.
Use workmat 3 and tens and ones blocks.

Check children's underlining.

1. Cora has 17 games at her house. She has 8 games at her grandmother's house. How many games does Cora have in all?

   17 (+) 8 (=) 25 games

2. Jody and his friends play with 24 toy trucks. They lose 5 of them in the sand box. How many toy trucks are left?

   24 (−) 5 (=) 19 toy trucks

3. There are 18 books on the shelf. People take 5 of the books to read. How many books are left?

   18 (−) 5 (=) 13 books

4. There are 12 people in the swimming pool. Then 10 more people jump in. How many people are in the pool now?

   12 (+) 10 (=) 22 people

Name ______________________________

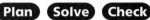

Understand Plan Solve Check

Subtract 1-Digit Numbers

Use Workmat 3 and 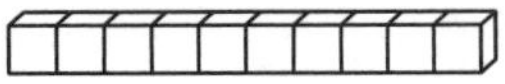 . Subtract.

1. Terry finds 17 shells. Amy finds 9 shells. How many more shells does Terry find?

   __8__ shells

2. There are 22 families on the beach. Then 8 families go home. How many families are left?

   __14__ families

3. There are 24 children swimming. 6 other children are making a sand castle. How many more children are swimming?

   __18__ children

4. Terry finds 14 shells before lunch. He finds 7 shells after lunch. How many more shells does he find before lunch?

   __7__ shells

5. Mark counts 32 fish. Maria counts 9 fish. How many more fish does Mark count?

   __23__ fish

6. Jean has 23 shells. She gives 5 shells to Tony. How many shells does Jean still have?

   __18__ shells

Mark the correct answer.

7.

	tens	ones
	□	□
	4	2
−		7

○ 33
● 35
○ 37
○ 40

8.

	tens	ones
	□	□
	6	7
−		8

○ 49
● 59
○ 61
○ 63

Name ____________________

LESSON 10.2

Understand Plan Solve Check

Subtract 2-Digit Numbers

Use Workmat 3 and 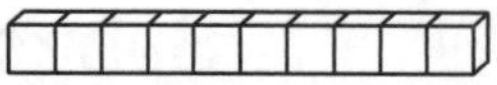 .
Solve.

Do your work here.

1. On Saturday morning 32 cars and 15 vans came to the car wash. How many more cars than vans came?

   __17__ more cars

   $$\begin{array}{r} \overset{2\ 12}{\cancel{3}\cancel{2}} \\ -\ 15 \\ \hline 17 \end{array}$$

2. One day 33 cars and 17 trucks are washed. How many more cars than trucks are washed?

   __16__ cars

   $$\begin{array}{r} \overset{2\ 13}{\cancel{3}\cancel{3}} \\ -17 \\ \hline 16 \end{array}$$

3. 32 cars were washed in the morning. 27 were washed in the afternoon. How many more cars were washed in the morning?

   __5__ cars

   $$\begin{array}{r} \overset{2\ 12}{\cancel{3}\cancel{2}} \\ -27 \\ \hline 5 \end{array}$$

Mark the correct answer.

4.

tens	ones
☐	☐
4	5
− 1	9

- ○ 36
- ○ 34
- ● 26
- ○ 24

5.

tens	ones
☐	☐
5	3
− 2	6

- ○ 17
- ● 27
- ○ 39
- ○ 43

Name ______________________

Understand Plan Solve Check

More 2-Digit Subtraction

Solve.

Do your work here.

1. Megan had 73 books at the garage sale. She sold 42. How many are left? 31 books	73 − 42 = 31
2. Cal has 24 toys for sale. He sells 16. How many are left? 8 toys	1 14 24 − 16 = 8
3. There were 24 garden tools for sale. Brenda bought 10. How many were left? 14 garden tools	24 − 10 = 14

Mark the correct answer.

4.

tens	ones
☐	☐
3	2
− 1	6

○ 14
● 16
○ 24
○ 26

5.

tens	ones
☐	☐
4	3
− 2	5

○ 13
○ 16
● 18
○ 28

Name ______________________

Understand Plan Solve Check

Rewrite 2-Digit Subtraction

Solve. Show your work. Do your work here.

1. There are 65 students on the playground. 47 are wearing sneakers. How many are not wearing sneakers?

   65 − 47 = ______

   18 students

tens	ones
5	15
6	5
− 4	7
1	8

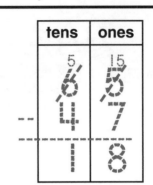

2. There are 83 students eating lunch. 55 are eating hot lunches. How many students are not eating hot lunches?

   83 − 55 = ______

   28 students

tens	ones
7	13
8	3
− 5	5
2	8

3. There are 50 students in the library at Martin Luther King, Jr. Elementary School. 27 of them are girls. How many are boys?

   50 − 27 = ______

   23 boys

4	10
5	0
− 2	7
2	3

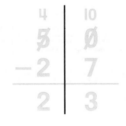

Mark the correct answer.

4. There are 30 teachers at City Elementary School. 14 of them are not wearing green today. How many of them are wearing green?

2	10
3	0
− 1	4
1	6

- ○ 24
- ○ 26
- ● 16
- ○ 44

Name ____________________

Understand Plan Solve Check

Estimate Differences

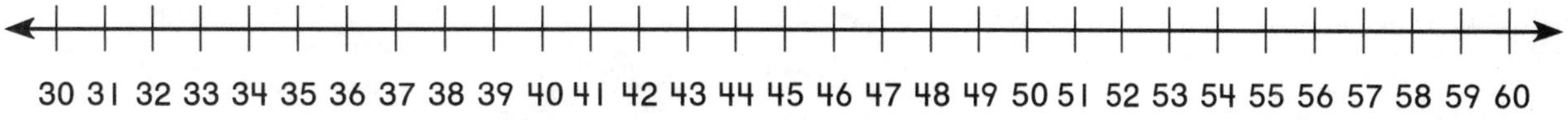

Use the number line to round each number to the nearest ten. Estimate the difference.

1. Morgan put 31 red beads and 42 blue beads on a string. About how many more blue beads did she use?

   about __10__ blue beads

2. Sherry chose 58 shells and 42 beads to make a necklace. About how many more shells did she choose?

   about __20__ shells

3. John needs 55 beads to make a key chain. He has 33 beads. About how many more beads does John need?

   about __30__ beads

Estimate the difference. Mark the correct answer

4. Bria's necklace has 57 white beads and 38 black beads. About how many more white beads are on the necklace?

   ○ 10 ○ 30
   ● 20 ○ 40

5. 45 beads fell on the floor. Clay picked up 35 of them. About how many more beads are still on the floor?

   ● 10 ○ 30
   ○ 20 ○ 40

Name ______________________

Understand Plan Solve Check

Algebra: Use Addition to Check Subtraction

Subtract.
Add to check.

1. Devin cut out 74 snowflakes and 38 stars. How many more snowflakes than stars did he cut out? 36 more snowflakes	74 − 38 = 36 36 + 38 = 74
2. Zach made 61 moons. Jan made 9 moons. How many more moons did Zach make? 52 more moons	61 − 9 = 52 52 + 9 = 61
3. Lana wants 84 stars. She has made 37. How many more stars must she make? 47 more stars	84 − 37 = 47 47 + 37 = 84

Mark the correct answer.

4. Which numbers should you add to check the subtraction problem?

$$\begin{array}{r} 57 \\ -\ 25 \\ \hline 32 \end{array}$$

- ● $32 + 25$
- ○ $57 + 25$
- ○ $32 + 57$
- ○ $32 + 32$

Name ______________________

Understand Plan Solve Check

Reading Strategy: Words That Compare

Words that compare can help you solve problems.

Ben, Tani, and Mira are fast runners. At the track meet, Mira ran slower than Ben. Tani ran fastest of all. What place did each runner get?

1. Look for words that compare, such as *slower* and *fastest*. Underline the words.

2. Sentences that compare give you clues. Use each clue to place the runners in order.

   Tani ran fastest of all. is a good clue. What place did Tani get? first place

3. Solve the problem. Write who won each place.

Look for words that compare. Then solve.

4. Ray, Alex, and Jesse each built a sand castle. Jesse built the shortest castle. Ray's castle was shorter than Alex's, but taller than Jesse's. What is the order of the castles from tallest to shortest?

Alex ______ Ray ______ Jesse ______

tallest ⟷ shortest

Name ______________________

Understand Plan Solve Check

Different Ways to Add

Solve.

1. There were 17 people on one train. There were 30 people on another train. How many people were on both trains?

   47 people

2. Ramon bought a box of 24 pencils. His friend gave him 3 more pencils. How many pencils did Ramon have in all?

   27 pencils

3. Ms. Grant's class has 18 boys and 17 girls. How many children are in the class?

   35 children

4. There are 43 ducks and 30 geese at the pond. How many ducks and geese are at the pond in all?

   73 ducks and geese

5. Juan is making a bookcase. He needs 26 long nails and 26 short nails. How many nails does he need in all?

   52 nails

6. Mr. Hoi collects CDs of jazz music and rock music. He has 35 jazz CDs and 27 rock CDs. How many CDs does he have?

   62 CDs

Mark the correct answer.

7. 32 + 30 =
   - ○ 42
   - ○ 52
   - ● 62
   - ○ 72

8. 48 + 27 =
   - ○ 64
   - ○ 65
   - ○ 74
   - ● 75

Name ______________________________

Understand Plan Solve Check

Practice 2-Digit Addition

Marlee, Doug, Hector, and Troy are in a swim club. The chart shows the number of laps each person swam last week. Use the chart to solve the problems.

Swimmer	Number of Laps
Marlee	35
Doug	14
Hector	46
Troy	19

1. How many laps did Marlee swim? How many laps did Doug swim? How many laps did they swim in all?

   Marlee: __35__ laps

   Doug: __14__ laps

   __49__ laps in all

2. How many laps did Hector swim? How many laps did Troy swim? How many laps did they swim in all?

   Hector: __46__ laps

   Troy: __19__ laps

   __65__ laps in all

3. How many laps did Marlee and Hector swim in all?

   __81__ laps

4. How many laps did Troy and Doug swim in all?

   __33__ laps

5. How many laps did Marlee and Troy swim in all?

   __54__ laps

6. How many laps did Hector and Doug swim in all?

   __60__ laps

Mark the correct answer.

7. Raul ran for 15 minutes. He biked for another 26 minutes. How many minutes did he spend running and biking?

   ○ 21 ○ 40
   ○ 31 ● 41

8. Nora made 23 saves in a soccer game. She made 19 saves in the next game. How many saves did she make in all?

   ○ 40 ● 42
   ○ 41 ○ 43

Name ______________________________

Understand | Plan | Solve | Check

Column Addition

Solve.

1. A street runs for three blocks. There are 14 houses on the first block. There are 18 houses on the second block. There are 24 houses on the third block. How many houses are on the street?

   56 houses

2. It takes Liat 15 minutes to eat breakfast, 25 minutes to eat lunch, and 35 minutes to eat dinner. How many minutes does it take him to eat all three meals?

   75 minutes

3. A bookcase has 3 shelves. The top shelf has 8 books, the middle shelf has 29 books, and the bottom shelf has 31 books. How many books are in the bookcase?

   68 books

4. Three friends knit scarves. Each scarf is 18 inches long. What is the total length of the scarves?

   54 inches

Add. Mark the correct answer.

5. $25 + 17 + 44 =$

   ○ 74 ○ 84
   ○ 76 ● 86

6. $14 + 19 + 29 =$

   ○ 52 ○ 72
   ● 62 ○ 82

Name ______________________

Understand Plan Solve Check

Different Ways to Subtract

Subtract using different ways.

1. Nat had 75 trading cards. He gave 3 away. How many trading cards does he have left?

72 trading cards

2. There were 27 birds in the tree. Then 18 flew away. How many birds were still in the tree?

9 birds

3. Karen has 34 bows. She gives 3 of them away. How many bows does she have left?

31 bows

4. There are 47 fish in the pond. There are 58 fish in the lake. How many more fish are in the lake?

11 fish

5. Valerie's basketball team scored 57 points. The other team scored 30 points. How many more points did Valerie's team score?

27 points

6. Lisa has 52 pennies in a box. She takes 18 of the pennies out and uses them to play a game. How many pennies are left in the box?

34 pennies

Mark the correct answer.

7. 55 − 10 =

- ○ 35
- ● 45
- ○ 50
- ○ 55

8. 61 − 28 =

- ● 33
- ○ 34
- ○ 43
- ○ 48

Name ____________________

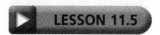

Understand Plan Solve Check

Practice 2-Digit Subtraction

Complete the subtraction sentence. Solve.

1. There are 47 chickens in the barn. 23 of them lay eggs. How many chickens do not lay eggs?

   47 – 23 = 24

   24 chickens

2. There are 22 sheep on the farm. 18 sheep are in the barn. How many sheep are not in the barn?

   22 – 18 = 4

   4 sheep

3. There are 56 cows in the barn. 20 cows give milk. How many cows do not give milk?

   56 – 20 = 36

   36 cows

4. There are 38 horses in the pasture. 15 are brown. How many horses are not brown?

   38 – 15 = 23

   23 horses

5. There are 26 pigs in the pen. 11 pigs have spots. How many pigs do not have spots?

   26 – 11 = 15

   15 pigs

6. There are 46 goats in the field. 26 are eating hay. How many goats are not eating hay?

   46 – 26 = 20

   20 goats

Mark the correct answer.

7. What is the difference for 93 – 52?

   ○ 40 ○ 48

   ● 41 ○ 51

8. What is the difference for 93 – 39?

   ○ 64 ● 54

   ○ 60 ○ 52

Understand Plan Solve Check

Mixed Practice

The chart shows the number of games each team won. Use the chart to solve the problems.

Team	Games Won
Bluebirds	24
Hawks	17
Robins	36
Crows	9

1. How many games did the Hawks and the Bluebirds win in all?

   41 games

2. How many more games did the Hawks win than the Crows?

   8 games

3. How many games did the Crows and the Robins win in all?

   45 games

4. How many more games did the Robins win than the Crows?

   27 games

5. How many games did the Bluebirds and the Robins win in all?

   60 games

6. How many more games did the Bluebirds win than the Hawks?

   7 games

Mark the correct answer.

7. 28 + 16 =
   - ○ 32
   - ○ 34
   - ○ 42
   - ● 44

8. 63 − 18 =
   - ○ 44
   - ● 45
   - ○ 54
   - ○ 55

Name ________________________

Understand Plan Solve Check

Reading Strategy: Sequence Events

Knowing the order in which things happen can help you solve math problems.

Greta had some buttons. First she gave 15 buttons to her sister. Then she gave 10 buttons to her brother. Now Greta has 28 buttons. How many buttons did she have to start?

1. First Greta gave 15 buttons to her sister.

2. Then she gave 10 buttons to her brother.

3. Now Greta has 28 buttons.

4. Solve by working backward.

28 buttons now	38 total buttons
+ 10 buttons to her brother	+ 15 buttons to her sister
38 total buttons	53 total buttons

Greta had 53 buttons at the start.

Think about the order in which things happen. Then solve.

5. Ilana had a bag of stickers. She gave 20 stickers to Fan and 8 stickers to Lou. That left 21 stickers in the bag. How many stickers were in the bag to start?

49 stickers

6. Harley collected some rocks in the morning. He collected 42 more rocks in the afternoon. He collected 71 rocks in all. How many rocks did he collect in the morning?

29 rocks

Name ______________________

LESSON 12.1

Understand **Plan** **Solve** **Check**

Pennies, Nickels, and Dimes

Count on to find the total amount.
Write the name of the toy that costs the same amount.

1.

bear

2.

mouse

3.

lion

Mark the correct answer.

4. Which is the total amount?

- ○ 7¢
- ● 8¢
- ○ 12¢
- ○ 13¢

5. Which is the total amount?

- ○ 7¢
- ○ 12¢
- ○ 17¢
- ● 22¢

Name ____________________

Understand Plan Solve Check

Quarters and Half-Dollars

Draw coins to solve.

Check children's work.

1. Wayne has 1 half-dollar, 3 nickels, and 2 pennies.
   How much money does he have?

   50¢ 5¢ 5¢ 5¢ 1¢ 1¢ — 67 ¢

2. Amy has 1 quarter and 4 nickels.
   How much money does she have?

   25¢ 5¢ 5¢ 5¢ 5¢ — 45 ¢

3. Leon has 1 half-dollar, 1 quarter, and 4 pennies.
   How much money does he have?

   50¢ 25¢ 1¢ 1¢ 1¢ 1¢ — 79 ¢

Mark the correct answer.

4. Which is the total amount?

○ 95¢ ○ 90¢
● 85¢ ○ not here

5. Which is the total amount?

○ 71¢ ○ 66¢
● 61¢ ○ not here

Name ______________________________

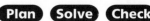

Understand Plan Solve Check

Count Collections

Think of a way to solve each problem.

Check children's work.

1. Mei had these coins.

She spent 1 quarter. How much money did she have left? __21__ ¢

2. These coins are in Roger's bank.

Roger adds 1 nickel. How much money is in Roger's bank now? __85__ ¢

3. Dorothy has these coins.

She gets another coin. Now she has 50¢. What coin did she get? __a nickel__

Mark the correct answer.

4. Which is the total amount?

- ◯ 36¢ (marked)
- ◯ 41¢
- ◯ 46¢
- ◯ 51¢

5. Which is the total amount?

- ◯ 20¢
- ◯ 17¢
- ◯ 22¢
- ◯ 16¢ (marked)

Name ______________________________

Understand Plan Solve Check

1 Dollar

Draw and label coins to solve.

Check children's drawings.

1. Bruce has 11 coins that equal $1.00. Some are dimes. Some are nickels. How many of each coin does he have?

   __9__ dimes __2__ nickels

2. Antonio has 11 coins that equal $1.00. Some are half-dollars. Some are nickels. How many of each coin does Antonio have?

   __1__ half-dollar __10__ nickels

3. Neil has 8 coins that equal $1.00. Some are quarters. Some are nickels. How many of each coin does Neil have?

   __3__ quarters __5__ nickels

Mark the correct answer.

4. How many 

equal $1.00?

   ○ 2 ○ 10

   ● 4 ○ 25

5. How many 

equal $1.00?

   ○ 2 ○ 10

   ○ 4 ● 20

Name ______________________________

LESSON 12.5

Understand Plan Solve Check

Add Money

Solve.

1. Gil buys a carrot for 25¢. He buys a tomato for 55¢. How much money does he spend altogether?

   80¢

2. Kareem has 22¢ in one pocket. He has 49¢ in another pocket. How much money does he have in all?

   71¢

3. Vijay's family has a yard sale. He sells one toy car for 38¢ and another for a nickel. How much money does he get in all?

   43¢

4. Kristin finds 9¢ one morning. She finds 37¢ two days later. How much money does she find in all?

   46¢

5. Ms. Bowers buys a newspaper and a postcard. The newspaper costs 35¢. The postcard costs a quarter. How much money does she spend in all?

   60¢

6. Serena has 48¢ in her piggy bank. She add 2 quarters to the bank. How much money does she have in her bank now?

   98¢

Mark the correct answer.

7. 45¢ + 38¢

   - ○ 73¢
   - ○ 85¢
   - ● 83¢
   - ○ 93¢

8. 27¢ + 14¢

   - ○ 31¢
   - ● 41¢
   - ○ 32¢
   - ○ 42¢

Name ______________________________

Understand Plan Solve Check

Reading Strategy • Use Graphic Aids

Jack has 8 coins. They are dimes and nickels. He has more dimes than nickels. What coins could Jack have?

You can use a chart to solve the problem.

Dimes	Nickels	Total
7	1	75¢
6	2	70¢
5	3	65¢

1. Which combination of coins has the greatest value? 7 dimes 1 nickel

2. Which combination of coins has the least value? 5 dimes 3 nickels

3. Tanya has 7 coins. She has only quarters and pennies. She has more pennies than quarters. What coins could Tanya have?

Quarters	Pennies	Total
1	6	31¢
2	5	55¢
3	4	79¢

4. Which combination of coins has the greatest value? 3 quarters 4 pennies

5. Which combination of coins has the least value? 1 quarter 6 pennies

Name ______________________

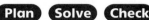

Understand Plan Solve Check

Make the Same Amounts

Draw and label the coins.
Write the amount.

Check children's drawings.

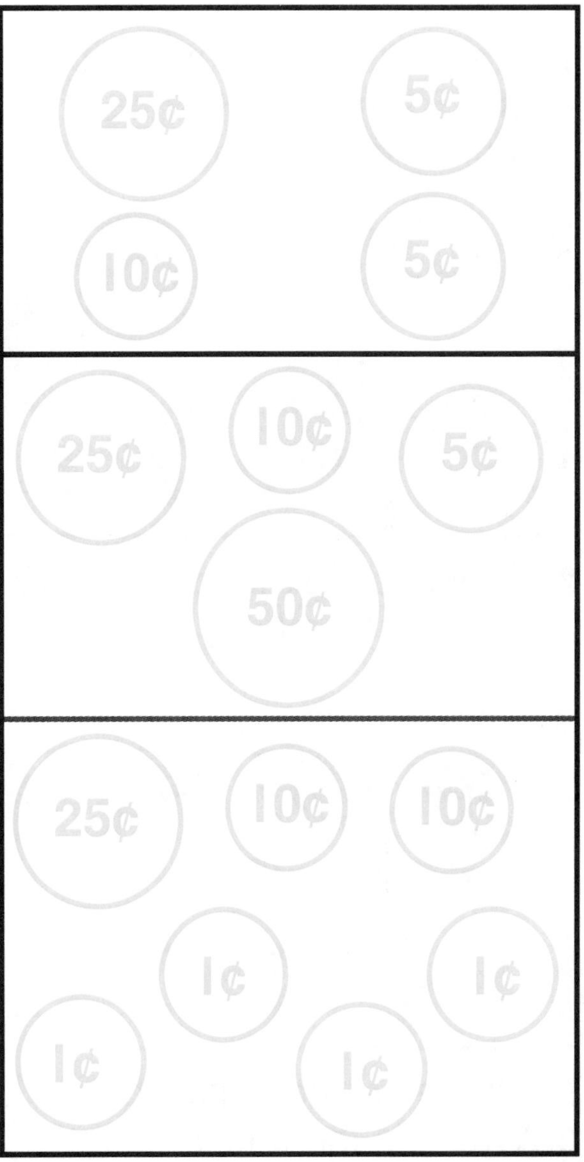

1. Greg has 15¢. His father gives him 30¢. How much money does Greg have now?

   45 ¢

2. Judy has 40¢. She earns 50¢ raking leaves. How much money does she have now?

   90 ¢

3. Bob has 1 quarter, 2 dimes, and 4 pennies. How much money does he have?

   49 ¢

Mark the correct answer.

4. Which is the total amount?

- ○ 55¢
- ○ 40¢
- ○ 35¢
- ● 31¢

Name ______________________________ LESSON 13.2

Understand Plan Solve Check

Algebra: Same Amounts Using the Fewest Coins

Solve. Then draw coins to show the same amount with the fewest coins. Label each coin.

Check children's drawings.

1. Allen has 1 quarter, 1 nickel, and 5 pennies. How much money does he have?

35 ¢

2. Paul has 4 dimes and 2 nickels. How much money does he have?

50 ¢

Mark the correct answer.

3. Which is the total amount?

- ◯ 50¢
- ● 35¢
- ◯ 30¢
- ◯ 26¢

4. Which is the total amount?

- ◯ 40¢
- ◯ 45¢
- ● 46¢
- ◯ 55¢

Name ______________________

Understand Plan Solve Check

Compare Amounts

Solve.

1. Mara has 1 quarter, 1 dime, and 1 nickel. Joe has 3 dimes and 1 nickel. Who has the greater amount?

   Mara

2. Elroy has 1 half dollar and 2 dimes. Toby has 1 quarter, 3 dimes, and 2 nickels. Who has the lesser amount?

   Toby

3. Kisha has 3 dimes, 2 nickels, and 5 pennies. Lucy has 1 quarter and 4 nickels. Do they have the same amount or different amounts?

   same amount

4. Flo has 1 quarter, 2 dimes, and 1 nickel. Luis has 1 half dollar and 3 nickels. Do they have the same amount or different amounts?

   different amounts

5. Taro has 2 dimes, 4 nickels, and 3 pennies. Ben has 1 quarter, 1 nickel, and 4 pennies. Who has the greater amount?

   Taro

6. Kari has 2 quarters, 1 dime, and 1 nickel. Mary has 1 quarter, 3 dimes, and 1 nickel. Who has the lesser amount?

   Mary

Mark your answer.

7. Which of the following is equal to 35¢?

   - ● 1 quarter, 1 dime
   - ○ 2 dimes, 1 nickel
   - ○ 5 nickels
   - ○ 1 dime, 4 nickels

8. Which of the following is less than 20¢.

   - ○ 2 dimes
   - ● 1 dime, 1 nickel
   - ○ 5 nickels
   - ○ 1 dime, 4 nickels

Understand Plan Solve Check

Compare Amounts to Prices

Write the names and prices of toys the child might buy.

Answers will vary. Possible answers are given.

1. Sally has 65¢.

cat 45¢

turtle 55¢

2. Alex has 95¢.

duck 85¢

fish 95¢

3. Terry has 80¢.

dog 70¢

cat 45¢

4. James has 75¢.

cat 45¢

turtle 55¢

Mark the correct answer.

5. Brad has

Does he have enough to buy a toy that costs 60¢?

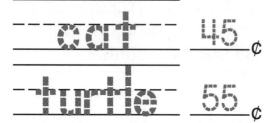

○ yes ○ no

Understand Plan Solve Check

Make Change to $1.00

Use coins to solve.

1. Jake has 40¢. He buys apple juice for 37¢. How much change does he get?

   3 ¢

2. Kelly has 81¢. She buys a muffin for 79¢. How much change does she get?

   2 ¢

3. Kay has 2 quarters, 2 nickels, and 6 pennies. Does she have enough money to buy a pen for 65¢?

   (Yes) No

4. Gino has 1 half-dollar, 1 quarter, 1 dime, and 1 nickel. How much money does he have?

   90 ¢

5. Les has 3 quarters, 1 dime, and 4 pennies. How much money does he have?

   89 ¢

6. Julie has 3 dimes, 4 nickels, and 5 pennies. How much money does she have?

   55 ¢

Mark the correct answer.

7. You have 46¢.
   You buy a toy car for 42¢.
   Your change is ______.

   - ○ 2¢
   - ○ 3¢
   - ● 4¢
   - ○ 5¢

8. You have 72¢.
   You buy a ball for 69¢.
   Your change is ______.

   - ○ 2¢
   - ● 3¢
   - ○ 4¢
   - ○ 5¢

Name ____________________

Understand Plan Solve Check

Subtract Money

Solve.

1. Allie buys a toy for 72¢. She has 95¢. How much change does she get?

   23 ¢

2. Steve has 47¢. Juan has 64¢. How much more money does Juan have?

   17 ¢

3. Malik has 35¢. He wants to buy a book for 87¢. How much more money does he need?

   52 ¢

4. Tara has saved 46¢. Maya has saved 39¢. How much money do they have altogether?

   85 ¢

5. Chelsea has 50¢. She buys a gift for 42¢. How much money does Chelsea have left?

   8 ¢

6. Mike has 22¢. Paul has 32¢ more than Mike. How much money does Paul have?

   54 ¢

Mark the correct answer.

7. Roberto has 75¢. He buys a ball for 59¢. How much change does he get?

   - ● 16¢
   - ○ 18¢
   - ○ 25¢
   - ○ 26¢

8. Diane has 37¢. Marie has 26¢. How much money do they have altogether?

   - ○ 11¢
   - ○ 21¢
   - ○ 53¢
   - ● 63¢

Name ______________________

Understand Plan Solve Check

Reading Strategy • Make Predictions

Sometimes a problem will ask you to tell if something can happen.

Mark has 85¢. He wants to buy a book about cars for 32¢. He wants to buy a book about cats for 47¢. Will Mark have enough money?

Estimate how much money Mark needs. 30¢ + 50¢ = 80¢

Will Mark have enough money? Yes, 80¢ < 85¢

Check your estimate. 32¢ + 47¢ = 79¢ 79¢ < 85¢

Solve. Make an estimate. Then circle yes or no.

1. John has 45¢. He wants to buy an apple for 16¢. He wants to buy an orange for 22¢. Will John have enough money?

   estimate: 40 ¢

   (yes) no

2. Rosa has 85¢. She wants to buy a ball for 43¢. She wants to buy a doll for 52¢. Will Rosa have enough money?

   estimate: 90 ¢

   yes (no)

3. Nancy sees a toy car that costs 19¢. She sees a toy boat that costs 33¢. Nancy has 65¢. Will she have enough money to buy the toys?

   estimate: 50 ¢

   (yes) no

4. Lahn wants a marker for 27¢. He wants some stickers for 39¢. Lahn has 60¢. Will he have enough money to buy the marker and stickers?

   estimate: 70 ¢

   yes (no)

Name ______________________________

LESSON 14.1

Understand Plan Solve Check

Explore 1 Minute

Solve.

1. Jo is going to weed her garden. Will it take her more than or less than 1 minute?

more than 1 minute

2. Kinja throws the ball into the basket. Does it take him more than or less than 1 minute?

less than 1 minute

3. Shana goes to a concert. Will the concert last more than or less than 1 minute?

more than 1 minute

4. Yoshi is going to write a letter to his grandmother. Will it take him more than or less than 1 minute?

more than 1 minute

5. Darnell can make 2 paper airplanes in 1 minute. How many paper airplanes can he make in 5 minutes?

10 paper airplanes

6. It takes 3 minutes for Dawn to walk around the playground. How many minutes will it take her to walk around the playground 2 times?

6 minutes

Solve.
Mark the correct answer.

7. Which takes less than 1 minute?

- pour a glass of water
- watch a movie
- read a book

8. Which takes more than 1 minute?

- wave to a friend
- snap your fingers
- eat lunch

Name ______________________________

Understand Plan Solve Check

Time to the Hour

Solve.

1. Billy practices soccer for one hour each day. If he starts at 3:00, what time will practice end?

   4:00

2. Tim leaves for school at 8:00 in the morning. He gets up one hour earlier. What time does Tim get up?

   7 o'clock

3. Rachel is watching a TV program. It started at 7:00. It will last for 1 hour. When will the program end?

   8:00

4. It takes 1 hour for Laura to get to her grandmother's house. She leaves at 10 o'clock in the morning. What time will she get there?

   11 o'clock

5. Kevin finished his homework at 5:00. He started one hour earlier. What time did Kevin start to do his homework?

   4:00

6. Lizzie went on a hike with friends. They left at 7:00 in the morning. They hiked for 2 hours. What time did the hike end?

   9 o'clock

Mark the correct answer.

7. Tony went to the park. He got there at 11:00 and stayed 1 hour. What time did he leave the park?

   ○ 10 o'clock
   ○ 11 o'clock
   ● 12 o'clock
   ○ 1 o'clock

8. Sue was at the library for 1 hour. She left the library at 11 o'clock. What time did she get to the library?

   ○ 9:00 o'clock
   ● 10:00 o'clock
   ○ 11:00 o'clock
   ○ 12:00 o'clock

Name ______________________

LESSON 14.3

Understand Plan Solve Check

Time to the Half-Hour

Solve.

1. May ate a peach at half past 6. What time was it when she ate the peach?

   6:30

2. The baseball game starts at 30 minutes after 1. What time does the baseball game start?

   1:30

3. Reya will stop reading her book at 30 minutes before 4. When will she stop reading her book?

   3:30

4. The Fowler family will leave for the park at five thirty. When will they leave for the park?

   5:30

5. Kenji starts watching a movie at 30 minutes before 1. What time is it when he starts watching the movie?

   12:30

6. Andy's art class starts at half past 10. What time was it when the class started?

   10:30

Solve.
Mark the best answer.

7. What is another name for 3:30?
   - ○ 30 minutes before 3
   - ● half past 3
   - ○ 30 minutes after 4
   - ○ none of these

8. What is another name for 10:30?
   - ○ 30 minutes after 9
   - ○ 30 minutes before 10
   - ○ half past 11
   - ● none of these

Name ____________________

Understand Plan Solve Check

Time to 15 Minutes

Solve.

1. Eric gets to the pool at 11:00 and starts swimming. He swims for 30 minutes. What time is it when he stops swimming?

   11:30

2. Mary starts reading her book at 8 o'clock. She stops reading 45 minutes later. What time is it when she stops reading?

   8:45

3. Terry took his dog for a walk at 4:00. They walked for 15 minutes. What time was it when they finished walking?

   4:15

4. It takes Harry 15 minutes to get ready for school. If he starts at 7 o'clock, what time will he be ready?

   7:15

5. Mark looked at the clock. The hour hand pointed a little past the 8. The minute hand pointed to 3. What time was it?

   8:15

6. Andy looked at his watch. The hour hand pointed halfway between the 2 and 3. The minute hand pointed to 6. What time was it?

   2:30

Solve.
Mark the best answer.

7. What time comes before 8:15?

   - ● 8:00
   - ○ 8:30
   - ○ 8:45
   - ○ 9:00

8. What time comes after 10:30?

   - ○ 9:45
   - ○ 10:00
   - ○ 10:15
   - ● 10:45

Minutes

Solve.

1. Grady feeds his cat when the clock says 4:42. Draw the minute hand on the clock to show the time.

2. Alan calls his friend when the clock says 2:25. Draw the minute hand on the clock to show the time.

3. Tracy turns on the radio at 7:16. Draw the minute hand on the clock to show the time.

4. At 10:08 LaToya goes out to weed the garden. Draw the minute hand on the clock to show the time.

Mark the correct answer.

5.

- ○ 2:42
- ● 3:28
- ● 3:42
- ○ 3:52

6.

- ○ 9:17
- ○ 10:12
- ○ 10:15
- ● 10:17

Name ____________________

Understand Plan Solve Check

Reading Strategy • Use Picture Clues

Using picture clues can help you solve problems.

Read the problem. Use the pictures to help you solve it.

Mr. Kim Leaves

Mr. Kim Gets Home

1. Mr. Kim goes to the supermarket at 10:00.
2. He gets home at 10:35.
3. How many minutes have passed? 35 minutes

Look for picture clues. Solve the problems.

Fran Leaves

Fran Gets Back

4. Fran goes for a walk.

   She leaves at 4:30.

   She comes back at 4:50.

   How many minutes have passed? 20 minutes

---

5. Barry starts playing soccer at 9:25.

   He stops playing at 11:25.

   How much time has passed?

   2 hours

Barry Starts Playing

Barry Stops Playing

Name ____________________

LESSON 15.1

Understand Plan Solve Check

Sequencing Months

Use the clues to name the month.

1. This month comes before April. This month begins with the letter J. What is the month?

   January

2. This month ends with the letter R. This month comes just before December. What is the month?

   November

3. This month comes before the eighth month but after the fifth month. It ends with the letter Y. What is the month?

   July

4. This month begins with the letter A. This month is not the eighth month. This month is just before May. What is the month?

   April

5. This month is 2 months before the eleventh month. This month is just after August. What is the month?

   September

6. The name of this month has 4 letters. This month is four months before October. What is the month?

   June

Mark the correct answer.

7. This month comes between September and December. This month does not begin with the letter *N*.

   - ○ January
   - ○ August
   - ● October
   - ○ November

8. This is the shortest month of the year. It comes between January and April. It has 8 letters in it's name.

   - ○ September
   - ○ November
   - ○ December
   - ● February

Name ______________________

LESSON 15.2

Understand Plan Solve Check

Dates on a calendar

Use the calendar to answer the questions.

April						
Sunday	Monday	Tuesday	Wednesday	Thursday	Friday	Saturday
	1	2	3	4	5	6
7	8	9	10	11	12	13
14	15	16	17	18	19	20
21	22	23	24	25	26	27
28	29	30				

1. Kara's first softball game is April 12. The next game is 11 days later. On what date is the next game?

   April 23

2. Anna's piano recital is on the third Friday. Kate's recital is 8 days after Anna's. On what date is Kate's recital?

   April 27

3. The first day of spring vacation is April 8. Students return to school 10 days later. What is the day and date that students return to school?

   Thursday

   April 18

4. Mona's soccer game is on the fourth Saturday. The soccer game before that was 12 days earlier. What are the dates of both games?

   April 27

   April 15

Mark the correct answer.

5. Jason's next piano lesson is 8 days after the first Wednesday. On what date is Jason's next lesson?

   ○ April 10 ○ April 12
   ● April 11 ○ April 15

6. Victor's next football game is a day before the last Monday. On what date is Victor's next game?

   ○ April 22 ○ April 27
   ○ April 25 ● April 28

Name ____________________

Understand Plan Solve Check

Days, Weeks, Months, Years

Use the clues to name the amount of time.

1. Miko's family goes on vacation for less than 3 weeks. Their vacation lasts more than 19 days. How many days is their vacation?

   20 days

2. Andy's baby brother is less than 1 year old. He is more than 10 months old. How many months old is Andy's brother?

   11 months

3. Alex's friend came to visit for more than 13 days. He visited for less than 15 days. How many weeks was the visit?

   2 weeks

4. Mary has lived in her house for less than 25 months. She has lived in her house for more than 23 months. How many years has Mary lived in her house?

   2 years

5. Arlene has been on the swim team for more than 1 month. She has been on the swim team for less than 6 weeks. How many weeks has Arlene been on the swim team?

   5 weeks

6. Anwar has been playing piano for more than 1 year. He has been playing for less than 14 months. How many months has Anwar been playing piano?

   13 months

Mark the correct answer.

7. A week more than 1 month is about ______?

   ○ 14 days ○ 8 weeks
   ● 5 weeks ○ 100 days

8. 53 weeks are a little more than ______?

   ○ 10 weeks ● 1 year
   ○ 6 months ○ 2 years

Name ______________________

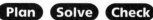

Understand Plan Solve Check

Estimate Time

Circle the best answer.

1. The Chin family is eating dinner right now. About how long will it take?

20 minutes 20 hours

2. Sam will mow the lawn today. About how long will it take him?

30 minutes 30 days

3. Jenna's baseball team has a game today. About how long will the game take?

2 hours 2 days

4. Melba's favorite TV show is starting. About how long is the show?

1 second 1 hour

5. Carmen is listening to her favorite tape. About how long will it take for her to listen to it?

60 minutes 60 hours

6. Raymond's family is going on vacation. About how long will they be gone?

10 days 10 years

Mark the correct answer.

7. About how long would it take to drive cross country?

- ○ 5 minutes
- ○ 5 days
- ○ 5 seconds
- ○ 5 years

8. About how long would it take to see a movie?

- ○ 2 hours
- ○ 2 months
- ○ 2 weeks
- ○ 2 seconds

Reading Strategy • Use Graphic Aids

Laura will be at a picnic all day on the second Friday of the month. She has a soccer game on the fourth Friday of the month. Can she take a dance lesson during the day on June 9?

June						
Sunday	Monday	Tuesday	Wednesday	Thursday	Friday	Saturday
				1	2	3
4	5	6	7	8	9	10
11	12	13	14	15	16	17
18	19	20	21	22	23	24
25	26	27	28	29	30	

What is the date of the second Friday?

June 9

What is the date of the fourth Friday?

June 23

Can Laura take a dance lesson on June 9? no

Why?

She has a picnic.

Use the calendar to solve.

1. Jacob has baseball practice on June 6, 13, and 20. What day of the week does Jacob have baseball practice?

Tuesday

2. Megan has piano lessons every Thursday. On what date is her last lesson in June?

June 29

3. Grace is going to a movie from noon until 3 P.M. on the third Saturday of the month. Can she visit her friend Mary at 1 P.M. on June 17? Why or why not?

no

She is going to a movie.

4. Tom has play practice all day on June 15. Can he go to a party during the day on the third Thursday of the month? Why or why not?

no

He has play practice.

Name ______________________

Understand | Plan | Solve | Check

Reading Strategy: Use Graphic Aids

You can use pictures, charts, and graphs to help you solve problems.

Mr. Dala's class sold T-shirts for the school. Four children sold the most shirts. How many more shirts did Perry sell than Anna?

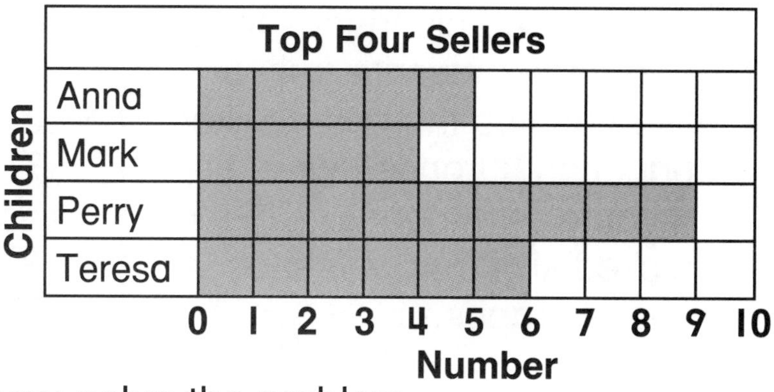

Use the bar graph to help you solve the problem.

1. How many T-shirts did Perry sell? 9
2. How many T-shirts did Anna sell? 5
3. How many more T-shirts did Perry sell than Anna? 9 − 5 = 4
4. Perry sold 4 more T-shirts.

Use the bar graph to solve.

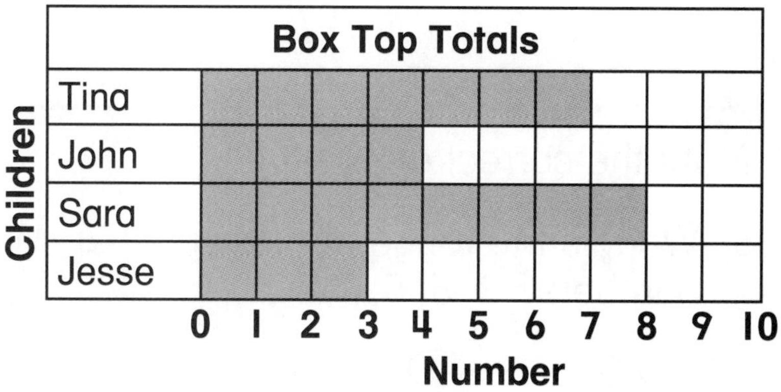

5. Miss Wallace's class collected box tops. Who collected the most box tops? Sara
6. Who collected the fewest box tops? Jesse
7. How many more box tops did Sara collect than John? 4
8. Who collected the second largest number of box tops? Tina

Name ___________________________

Understand Plan Solve Check

Range, Median, and Mode

Find the range, median, and mode for each group of numbers.

1. John asked his friends to name their favorite fruit. 5 liked apples the best. 3 liked bananas. Oranges were the favorite of 5 friends. 1 friend picked kiwi fruit. 2 friends chose grapes.

   range 4 median 3 mode 5

2. Ashley asked her classmates to name their favorite zoo animal. 11 chose monkeys. Tigers and elephants each were chosen 6 times. 3 children liked giraffes best. Tony said the iguana was his favorite.

   range 10 median 6 mode 6

3. Jim asked his classmates to name their favorite subject at school. 9 children chose art. 4 liked music. Another 4 children chose math. 5 liked science and 2 liked reading.

   range 7 median 4 mode 4

4. Kishi asked 20 people to name their favorite color. 3 people chose red. 6 people liked blue. Green was the favorite of 7 people. 3 liked yellow, and 1 liked orange.

   range 6 median 3 mode 3

Mark the correct answer.

5. What is the range of these numbers? 3, 5, 5, 7, 10

   ○ 3 ● 7
   ○ 5 ○ 10

6. What is the mode of these numbers? 5, 8, 8, 10, 12

   ○ 5 ○ 10
   ● 8 ○ 12

Understand Plan Solve Check

Algebra: Locate Points on a Grid

The grid shows places at the zoo.
Use the grid to answer the questions.

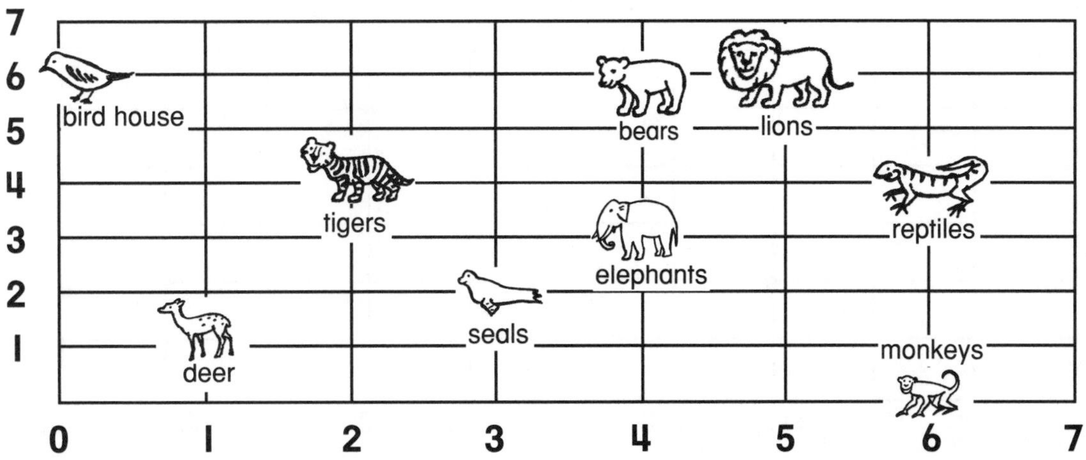

1. Mark and Jim walked past the deer. Where are the deer located?

   1,1 ______________

2. Kim wants to see the lions. Where are the lions located?

   5,6 ______________

3. Lucas wants to see the tigers. Where are the tigers located?

   2,4 ______________

4. Kito and Chet went to point 6,0. What is located there?

   monkeys ______________

5. Emma and Laura spent some time at point 3,2. What were they watching?

   seals ______________

6. Terry said he was going to walk to the bears. Where are the bears located?

   4,6 ______________

Mark the correct answer.

7. Where is the bird house located?

   ○ 0,6 ○ 6,0
   ○ 1,6 ○ 6,6

8. Where are the elephants located?

   ○ 3,4 ○ 4,4
   ○ 3,3 ○ 4,3

Name ______________________________

Understand Plan Solve Check

Read Line Graphs

Answer the questions and complete the line graph.

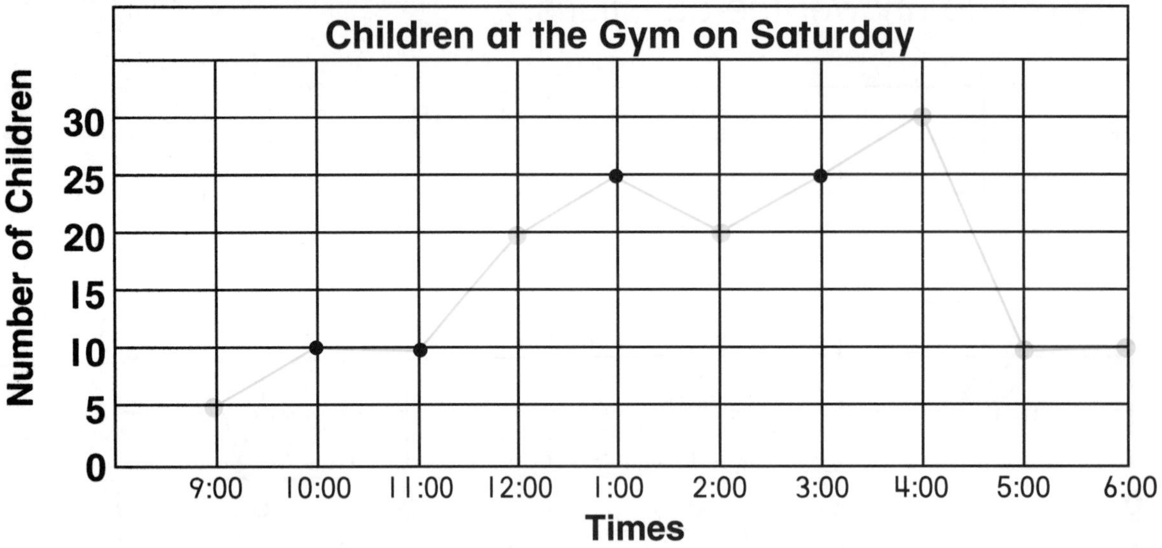

1. At 4:00, there were 20 more children than at 11:00. How many children were at the gym at 4:00?

30 children

2. There were 5 fewer children at 12:00 than at 1:00. How many children were at the gym at 12:00?

20 children

3. There were twice as many children at 2:00 as at 10:00. How many children were at the gym at 2:00?

20 children

4. The same number of children were at the gym at 5:00 and 10:00. How many children were there at 5:00?

10 children

Mark the correct answer.

5. There were 5 fewer children at 9:00 than at 5:00. How many children were at the gym at 9:00?

- (●) 5
- ( ) 10
- ( ) 15
- ( ) 20

6. There were 5 more children at 6:00 than at 9:00. How many children were at the gym at 6:00?

- ( ) 5
- (●) 10
- ( ) 15
- ( ) 20

Name ______________________

Understand Plan Solve Check

Reading Strategy: Make Predictions

Sometimes you will be asked to make a prediction based on a smaller group.

Tanya's aunt gave her a bag filled with quarters, dimes, nickels, and pennies. Tanya sorted a handful of coins. What prediction can she make about which coin there is the most of in the bag?

Coins Tanya Sorted	
Coin	**Tally**
quarter	||
dime	~~||||~~
nickel	|||
penny	~~||||~~ ~~||||~~

1. Compare the number of coins.

   quarters 2 dimes 5

   nickels 3 Pennies 10

2. Which coin is there the most of? penny

3. Which coin is there likely to be the most of in the bag?

   penny

Look at the tally table. Make a prediction.

4. Jamie grabbed a handful of marbles out of a bag. What prediction can he make about which color marble there are the fewest of?

   Prediction: The red marbles are the fewest.

Marbles in the Bag	
Color	**Tally**
blue	~~||||~~ |
red	||
green	~~||||~~
yellow	|||

5. What prediction can Jamie make about which color marble there are the most of?

   Prediction: The blue marbles are the most.

Name ______________________________

LESSON 17.1

Understand Plan Solve Check

Interpreting Outcomes of Games

Solve.

Drawings may vary. Possible drawings given.

1. Kamal made a spinner for which blue or red could be an outcome. Draw and color to show what Kamal's spinner might look like.

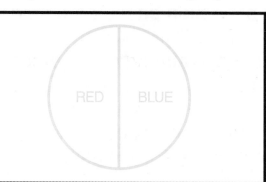

2. Ken made a spinner for which the outcome red occurred more often. Draw and color to show what Ken's spinner might look like.

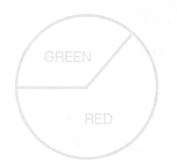

3. Jani made a spinner for which orange is one of three possible outcomes. Draw and color to show what Jani's spinner might look like.

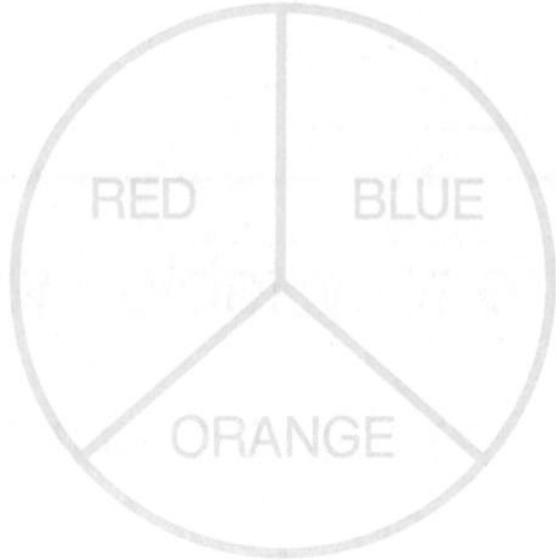

Mark the correct answer.

4. How many times was green the outcome?

○ 4　　○ 9
● 5　　○ 14

5. Which outcome occurred more often?

○ blue　　○ red
○ green　　● yellow

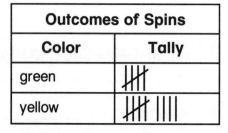

Outcomes of Spins	
Color	Tally
green	卌
yellow	卌 ||||

© Harcourt

Certain or Impossible

Circle **Yes** or **No**.

1. Sue has a bag with 14 green .
   Is pulling a green cube from the bag a certain outcome? **yes** (circled) no

2. Is pulling a yellow cube from Sue's bag an impossible outcome? **yes** (circled) no

3. Now Sue adds 3 yellow cubes to her bag. Is pulling a green cube a certain outcome? yes **no** (circled)

4. Is pulling a yellow cube a certain outcome? yes **no** (circled)

5. Is pulling a yellow cube an impossible outcome? yes **no** (circled)

6. How can you change the cubes in Sue's bag so that pulling a yellow cube is certain? Take out all the green cubes.

Mark the correct answer.

7.

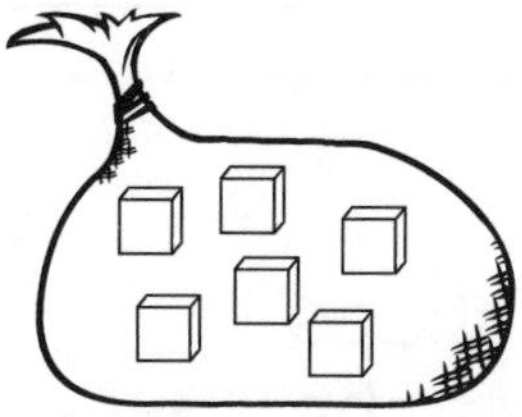

Which is a certain outcome?

- ○ pull a red cube
- ○ pull a gray cube
- ● pull a white cube

8.

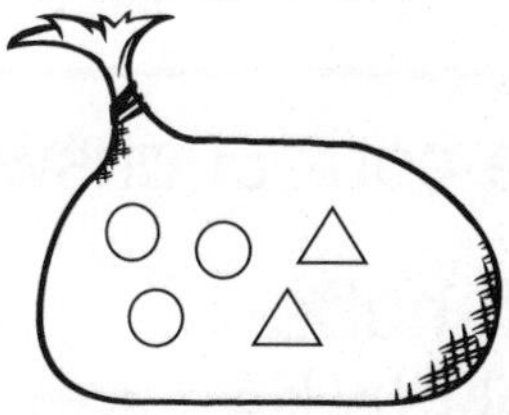

Which is an impossible outcome?

- ○ pull a circle
- ● pull a square
- ○ pull a triangle

Name ____________________

Understand Plan Solve Check

Likely and Unlikely

Solve.

1. Kayla has a bag with 8 squares and 2 triangles. Is she likely or unlikely to pull a square?

likely

2. Van has a bag with 7 yellow cubes and 1 orange cube. Is he likely or unlikely to pull an orange cube?

unlikely

3. Mike has a bag with 6 triangles and 2 squares. Mason has a bag with 5 squares and 1 triangle. Who is more likely to pull a triangle?

Mike

4. Faith has a bowl with 4 blue cubes and 1 yellow cube. Andy has a bowl with 5 yellow cubes and 2 blue cubes. Who is more likely to pull a blue cube?

Faith

5. Ruben is pulling a cube from a bowl with 5 yellow cubes, 3 green cubes, and 8 red cubes. Which color is Ruben likely to pull?

red

6. Elena has a bag with 3 triangles, 7 circles, and 4 squares. Which shape is she likely to pull?

circle

Mark the correct answer.

7. Which cube is likely to be pulled from the bag?

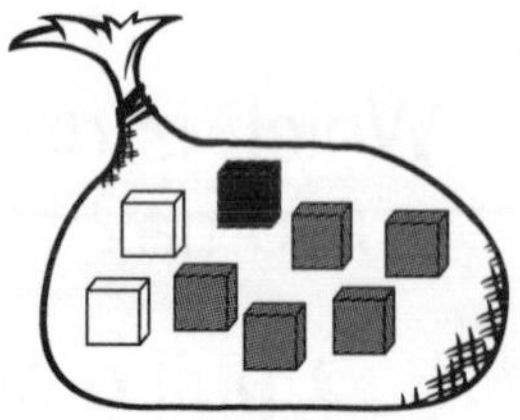

- gray
- white
- black

8. Which shape is likely to be pulled from the bag?

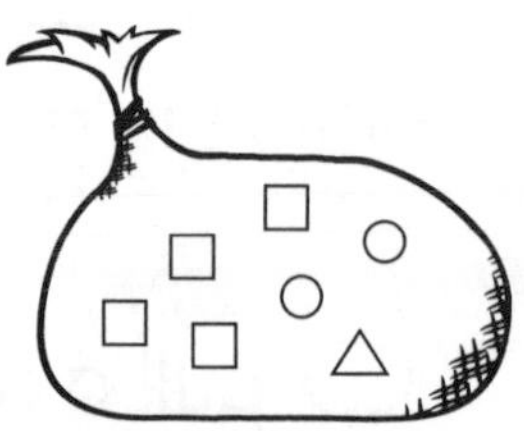

- circle
- square
- triangle

Understand Plan Solve Check

Likelihood of Events

Solve.

1. John has a bowl with 6 circles, 2 triangles, and 3 squares. Which shape is he most likely to pull from the bowl?

circle

2. Judy has a bag with 2 green marbles and 8 blue marbles. Which color is she more likely to pull from the bag?

blue

3. Cody has a drawer with 2 blue T-shirts, 1 white T-shirt, and 6 green T-shirts. If Cody grabs a T-shirt without looking, what color is it most likely to be?

green

4. Paula has a bag with 3 orange cubes and 7 blue cubes. Devin has a bag with 2 blue cubes and 6 orange cubes. Who is less likely to pull a blue cube?

Devin

5. Sara has a drawer with 6 pairs of white socks, 4 pairs of yellow socks, and 2 pairs of blue socks. If Sara grabs a pair of socks without looking, what color is it most likely to be?

white

6. Tim has 1 penny, 2 dimes, and 6 nickels in his pocket. If he takes out a coin without looking, what is it most likely to be?

nickel

Mark the correct answer.

7. Pulling a circle is _____.

- ○ most likely
- ● least likely
- ○ certain
- ○ impossible

8. Pulling a triangle is _____.

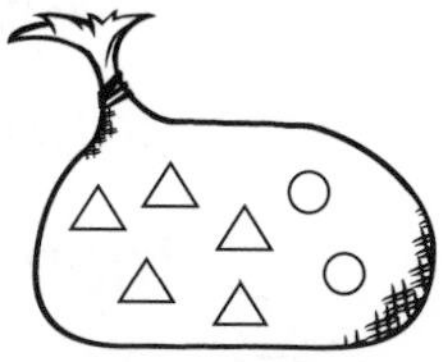

- ○ most likely
- ○ least likely
- ● more likely
- ○ less likely

Name ______________________________

LESSON 17.5

Understand Plan Solve Check

Equally Likely

Answers may vary. Sample answers are given.

Use the bag of shapes to answer the questions.

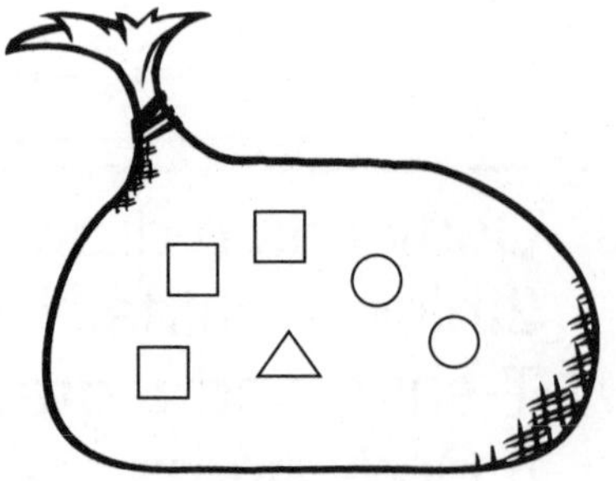

1. What could you change to make pulling a square and a triangle equally likely?

   Put in 2 more triangles.

   Take out 2 squares.

2. What could you change to make pulling a square less likely than pulling a circle?

   Put in 2 more circles.

   Take out 2 squares.

3. What could you change to make pulling a triangle more likely than pulling a square?

   Put in 4 more triangles.

   Put in 1 triangle and take out 2 squares.

Mark the correct answer.

4.

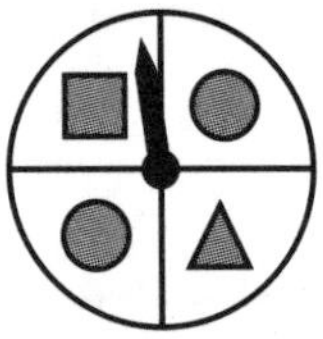

Which shapes are you equally likely to spin?

- triangle and square (marked)
- square and circle
- triangle and circle
- circle and rectangle

5.

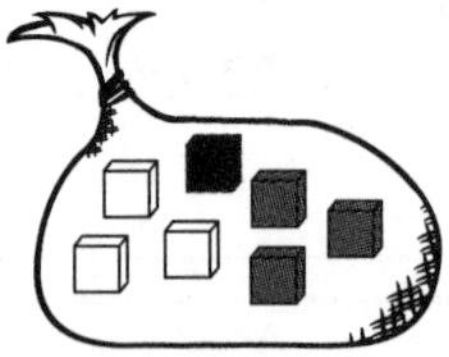

Which colors are equally likely to be pulled?

- black and gray
- gray and white (marked)
- black and white

Name ______________________________

Understand Plan Solve Check

Reading Strategy: Use Graphic Aids

Sometimes using a table or chart makes it easier to solve problems.

Nolan put the following shapes in a bag: square, circle, circle, triangle, square, triangle, square, circle, circle, circle, triangle, circle, circle, triangle, triangle. Which shape is most likely to be pulled?

1. Complete the tally table.

2. Look at the table. Which shape is most likely to be pulled from the bag?

circle

Shapes in the Bag	
Shape	**Tally**
circle	||||/ ||
square	|||
triangle	||||/

Make a table to solve.

3. Shelly put these shapes in a bag: circle, square, circle, circle, square, square, square, circle, square, and square. Which shape is more likely to be pulled?

Shapes in the Bag	
Shape	**Tally**
circles	||||
squares	||||/	

A square is more likely to be pulled.

4. Rico put these cubes in a box: blue, yellow, red, red, yellow, red, blue, red, yellow, yellow, red, blue, red, and red. Which color is most likely to be pulled?

Cubes in the Box	
Color	**Tally**
yellow	||||
red	||||/ ||
blue	|||

Red is most likely to be pulled.

Plane Shapes

Circle the correct shape.

1. Jerry is drawing a picture. He draws a circle for the sun. Which shape does he draw?

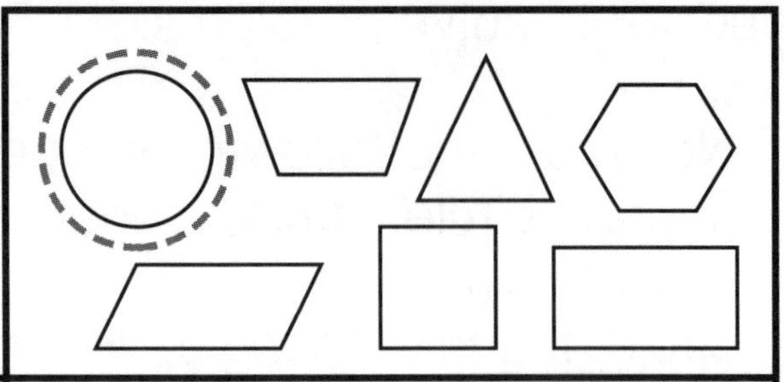

2. Meg is drawing a picture. She draws a triangle for a tree. Which shape does she draw?

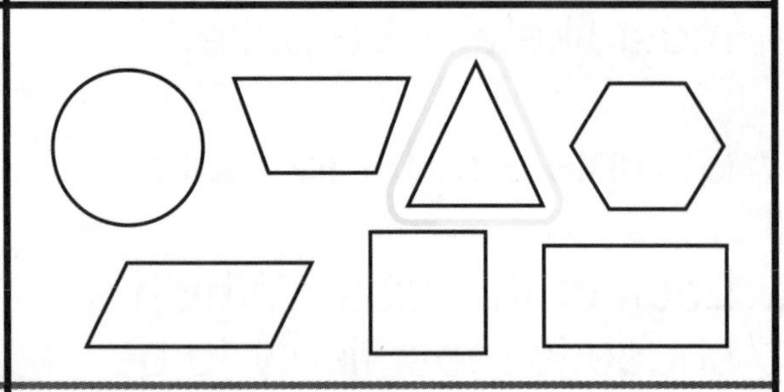

3. Marty is drawing a picture. He draws a trapezoid for a boat. Which shape does he draw?

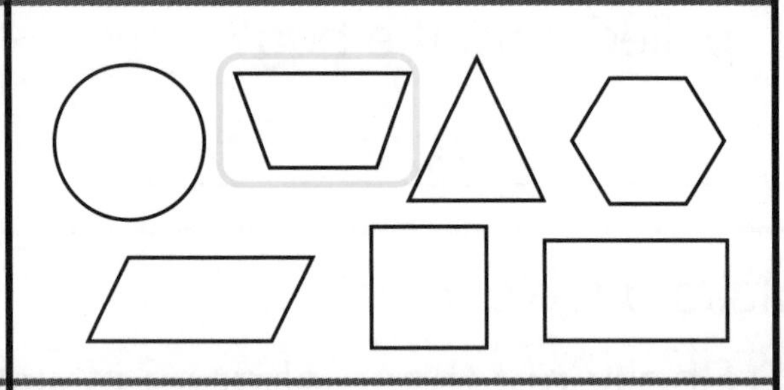

4. Lori is drawing a picture. She draws a square for a window. Which shape does she draw?

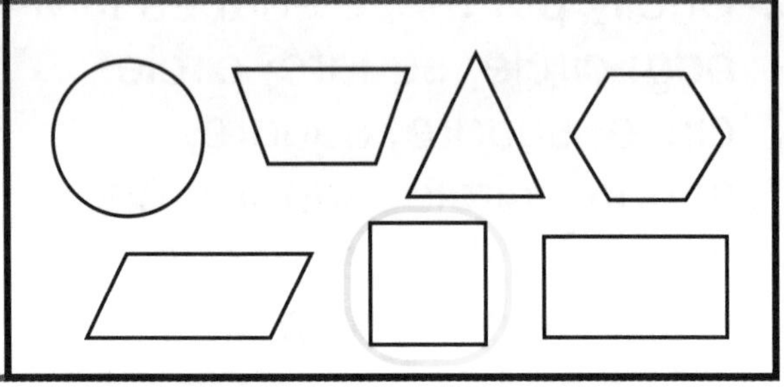

Mark the correct answer.

5. Which is a hexagon?

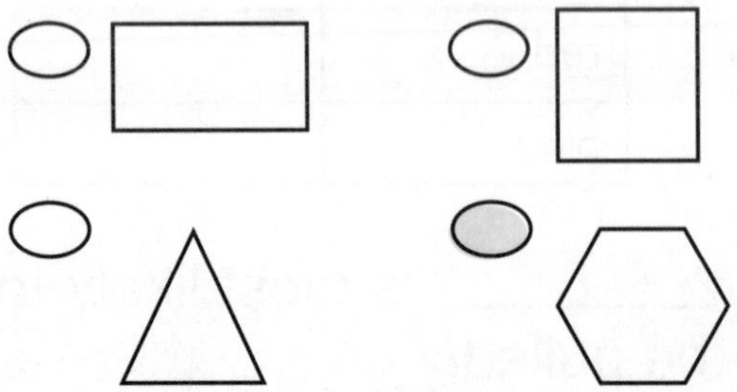

6. Which is a parallelogram?

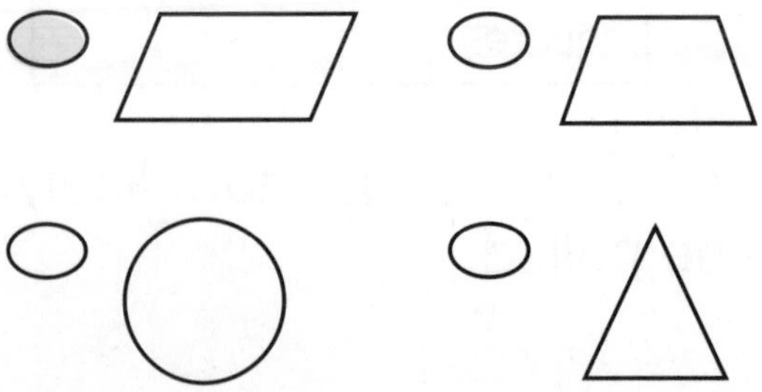

Name ____________________

Understand Plan Solve Check

Algebra: Sort Plane Shapes

Solve.

1. Sika has a right triangle, a circle, a square, and a rectangle. Which shape does not belong in a group named "Shapes with Square Corners"?

   circle

2. Taka has a hexagon, a triangle, a parallelogram, and a trapezoid. Which shape does not belong to a group named "Shapes with More Than 3 Angles"?

   triangle

3. Ramon has a trapezoid, a hexagon, a square, and a parallelogram. Which shape does not belong to a group named "Shapes with 4 Sides"?

   hexagon

4. Cody has a hexagon, a trapezoid, a rectangle, and a parallelogram. Which shape does not belong to a group named "Shapes with No Square Corners"?

   rectangle

5. April has a rectangle, a trapezoid, and a square. Circle the name she can give her group of shapes.

   Shapes with More Than 3 Sides

   Shapes with 3 Angles

6. Rosa has a trapezoid, a parallelogram, and a rectangle. Circle the name she can give her group of shapes.

   Shapes with Less Than 4 Sides

   Shapes with 4 Angles

Mark the correct answer.

7. What shape **does not** belong in the group "Shapes with Angles"?

   ○ hexagon
   ● circle
   ○ parallelogram

8. What shape **does** belong in the group "Shapes with More Than 4 Sides"?

   ○ triangle
   ○ rectangle
   ● hexagon

Name ______________________________

Understand Plan Solve Check

Combine and Separate Shapes

Circle the shape.

1. Tony has 2 triangles that are the same size and shape. What other shape could he make with the 2 triangles?

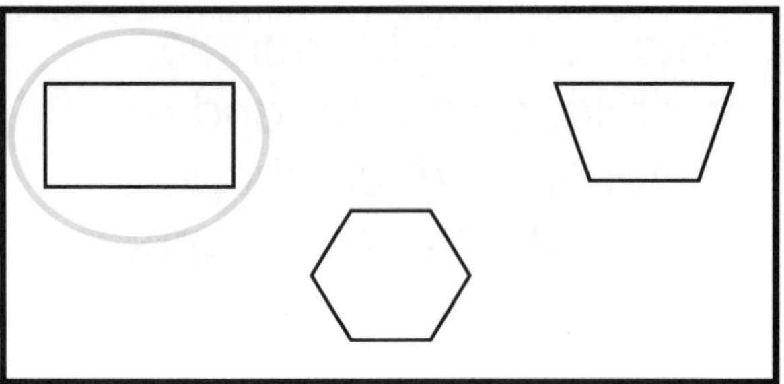

2. Norma has 3 parallelograms that are all the same shape and size. What other shape could she make with the 3 parallelograms?

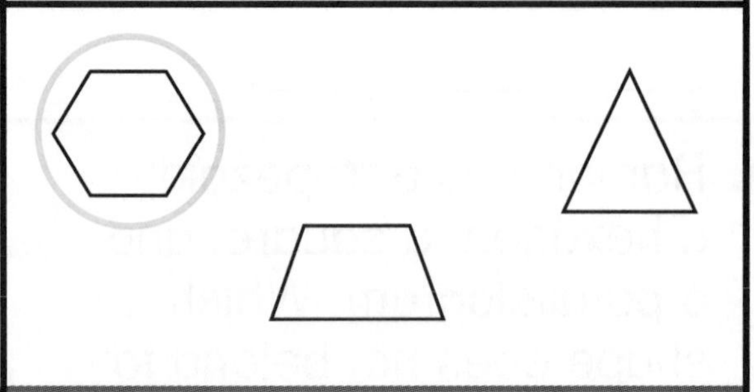

3. Kim has 3 triangles that are all the same shape and size. What other shape could she make with the 3 triangles?

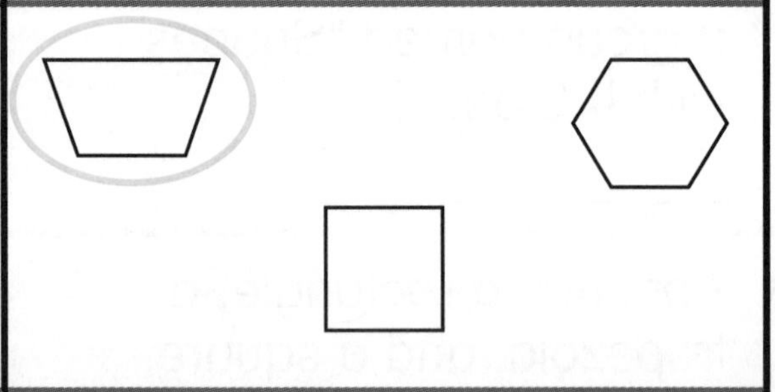

4. Scott has 3 triangles that are all the same size and shape. He also has 1 trapezoid. What other shape could he make with the triangles and trapezoid?

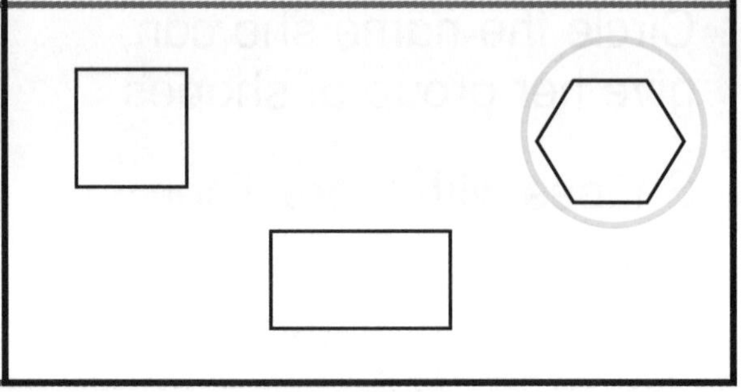

Mark the correct answer.

5. Which shapes can be used to make a trapezoid?
   - ● 3 triangles
   - ○ 2 hexagons
   - ○ 2 rectangles
   - ○ 3 squares

6. Which shapes can be used to make a hexagon?
   - ○ 2 squares
   - ○ 2 parallelograms
   - ○ 2 triangles
   - ● 2 trapezoids

Name ______________________

Understand Plan Solve Check

Reading Strategy • Create Mental Images

Ollie has 6 parallelograms.
How many hexagons can he make?

Picture the problem.

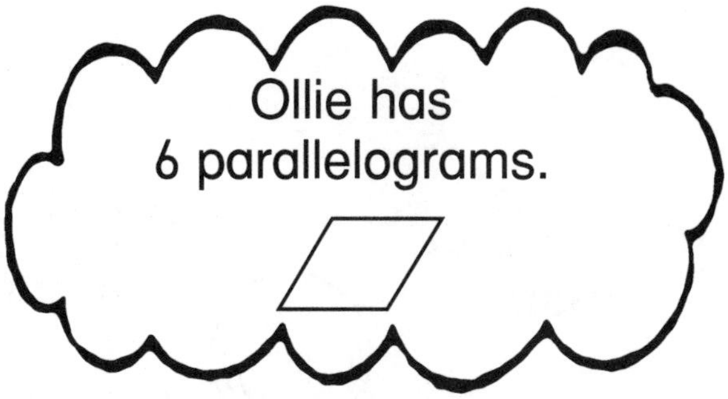
Ollie has
6 parallelograms.

Think about what you need to model.

Ollie needs
3 parallelograms to
make 1 hexagon.

Solve. Ollie needs ___3___ parallelograms for each hexagon.

Ollie can make ___2___ hexagons.

Picture the problems.
Then solve.

1. Fran has 8 trapezoids all the same size and shape. How many hexagons can she make with the 8 trapezoids?

   ___4___ hexagons

2. Shari has 2 squares that are the same size. She puts them together one above the other. What shape does she make?

   ___rectangle___

3. Frank has 12 triangles all the same shape and size. How many hexagons can he make with the 12 triangles?

   ___2___ hexagons

4. Joe has 8 triangles all the same size and shape. How many rectangles can he make with the 8 triangles?

   ___4___ rectangles

Name ______________________

Understand Plan Solve Check

Solid Figures

Write the name of the solid figure.

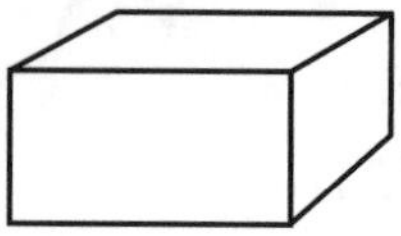

rectangular prism

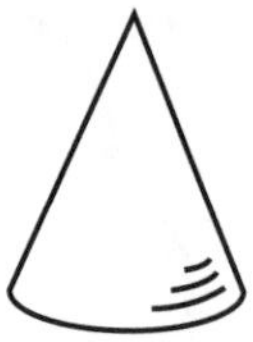

cone

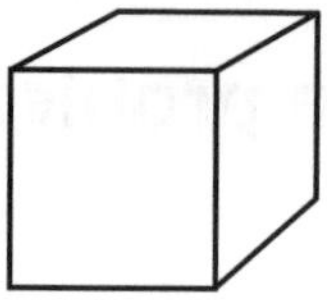

cube

sphere

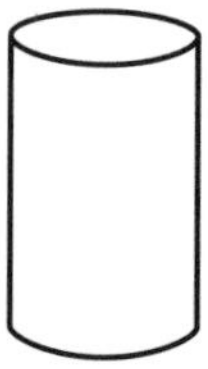

cylinder

pyramid

1. I am a can.
I am a drum.
What solid figure am I?

cylinder

2. I am a tepee.
I am a party hat.
What solid figure am I?

cone

3. I am a globe.
I am a beach ball.
What solid figure am I?

sphere

4. I am a shoe box.
I am a book.
What solid figure am I?

rectangular prism

Mark the correct answer.

5. Which object is shaped like this solid figure?

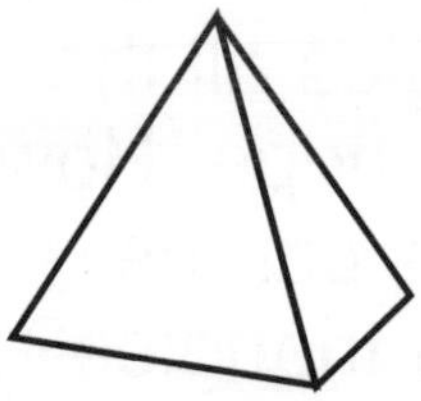

○ 

○ 

● 

6. Which object has the same shape as this solid figure?

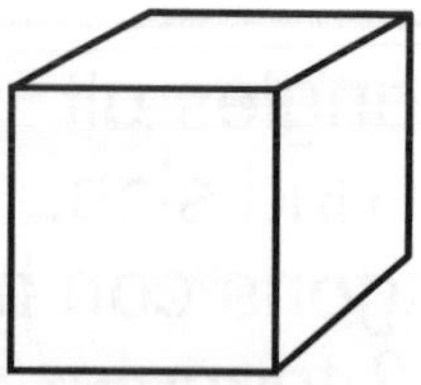

○ 

● 

○ 

Algebra: Sort Solid Figures

Circle the correct figures using the descriptions.

1. 0 faces, 0 edges, 0 corners

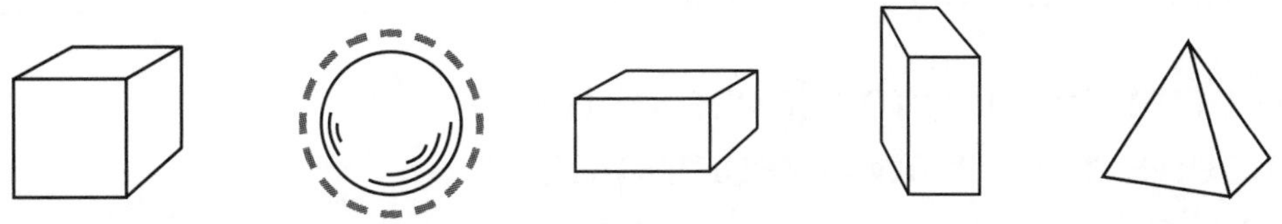

2. 6 faces, 12 edges, 8 corners

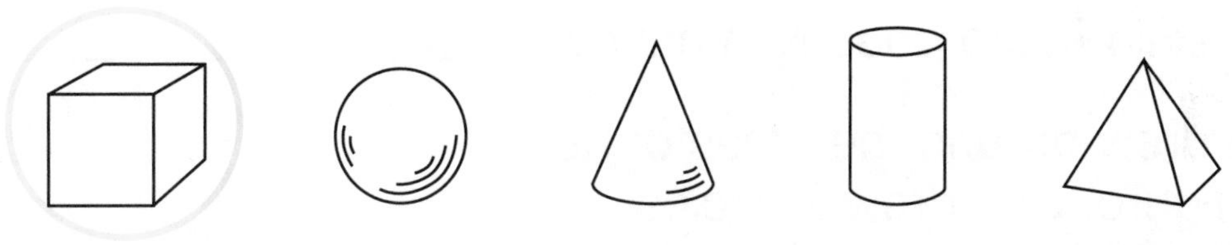

3. 5 faces, 8 edges, 5 corners

Mark the correct answer.

4. There is a figure with 5 faces, 8 edges, and 5 corners. Which is it?

5. There is a figure with 6 faces, 12 edges, and 8 corners. Which is it?

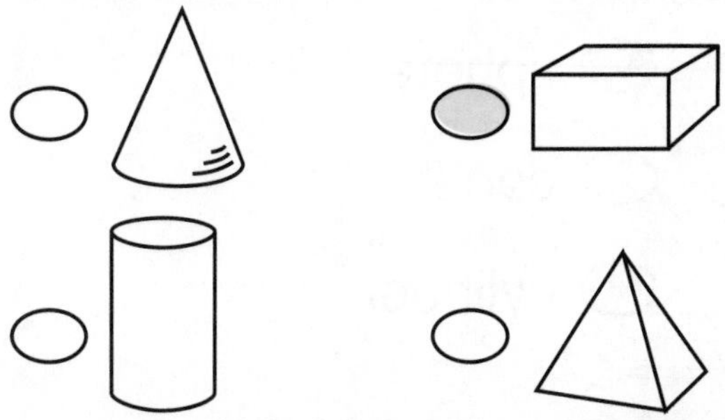

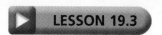

Understand Plan Solve Check

Compare Solid Figures and Plane Shapes

Write the name of the solid figure.

1. Taj drew around the faces of his solid figure. He drew 6 squares. What solid figure does Taj have? cube

2. Kyoko drew around the faces of her solid figure. She drew 6 rectangles. What solid figure does Kyoko have? rectangular prism

3. Ken drew around the faces of his solid figure. He drew 1 square and 4 triangles. What solid figure does Ken have? pyramid

4. Dena drew around the faces of her solid figure. She drew 2 circles. What solid figure does Dena have? cylinder

5. Omar drew around the only flat face of his solid figure. He drew 1 circle. What solid figure does Omar have? cone

Mark the correct answer.

6. Anna's solid figure does not have any faces to draw. What figure does she have?
   - ○ cube
   - ● sphere
   - ○ cone
   - ○ cylinder

7. Bo has two solid figures. They each have a square for one of their faces. Which two figures could she have?
   - ● pyramid and cube
   - ○ rectangular prism and cone
   - ○ sphere and cube
   - ○ cylinder and pyramid

Name ______________________________________

Understand Plan Solve Check

Reading Strategy: Use Graphic Aids

Sometimes you can use a table, chart, or graph to help you solve problems. Tables, charts, and graphs are called graphic aids.

This table shows the number of faces, edges, and corners for each solid figure.

Solid figure	Number of faces	Number of edges	Number of corners
cube	6 faces	12 edges	8 corners
sphere	0 faces	0 edges	0 corners
pyramid	5 faces	8 edges	5 corners
rectangular prism	6 faces	12 edges	8 corners

Use the information in the table to complete each problem.

1. A cube has ______6______ faces.

2. A rectangular prism has ______8______ corners.

3. A pyramid has ______8______ edges.

4. A ______sphere______ has 0 edges.

5. Both a ______cube______ and a ______rectangular prism______ have 12 edges.

6. A ______pyramid______ has 5 faces and 5 corners.

Name ____________________

LESSON 20.1

Understand Plan Solve Check

Congruence

Circle the correct answer.

1. Lily made 2 congruent triangles. Which triangles did Lily make?

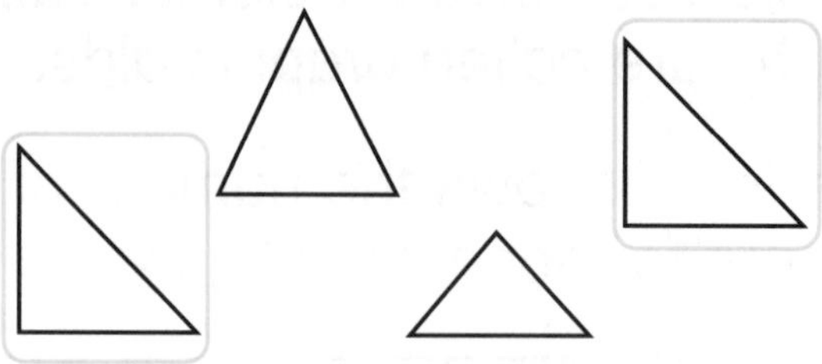

2. Ryan drew 2 congruent leaves. Which leaves did Ryan draw?

3. Karla finds 2 congruent seashells. Which seashells does Karla find?

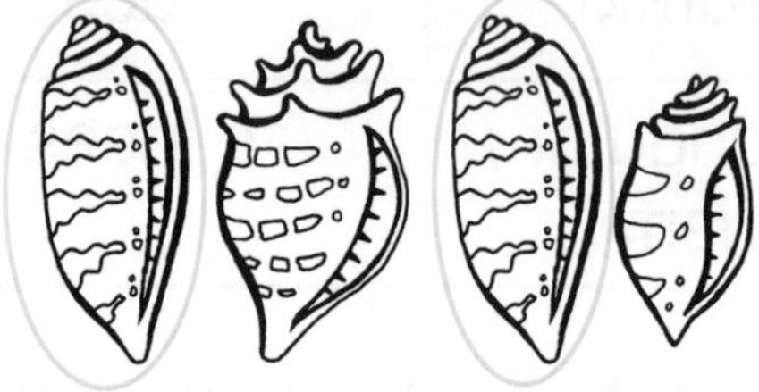

4. Tony has 2 congruent heart shapes. Which shapes does Tony have?

Mark the correct answer.

5. Which figure is congruent to ?

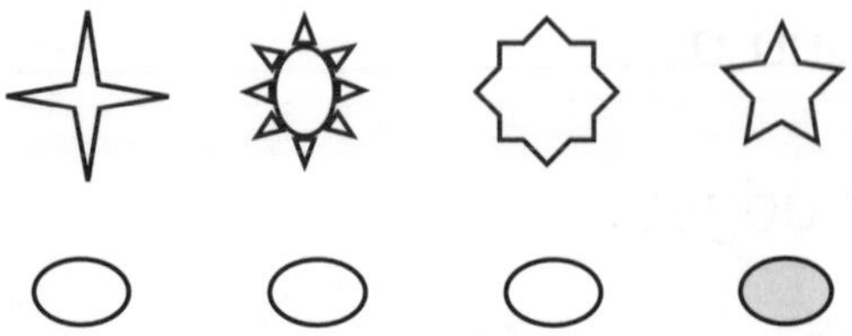

6. Which figure is congruent to ?

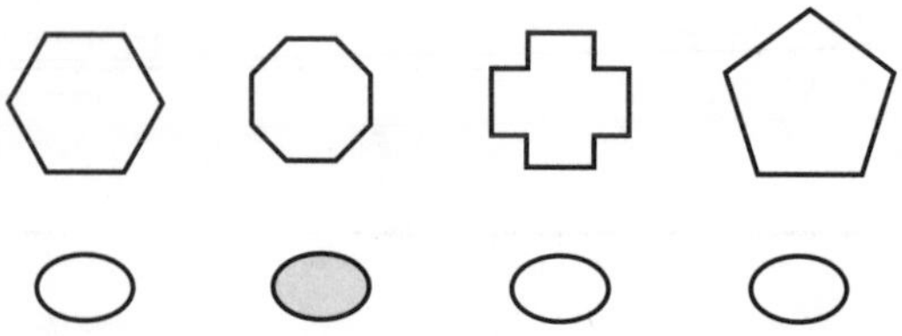

Name ______________________________

Symmetry

Circle the correct answer.

1. Peter drew a moon with a line of symmetry. Which moon did he draw?

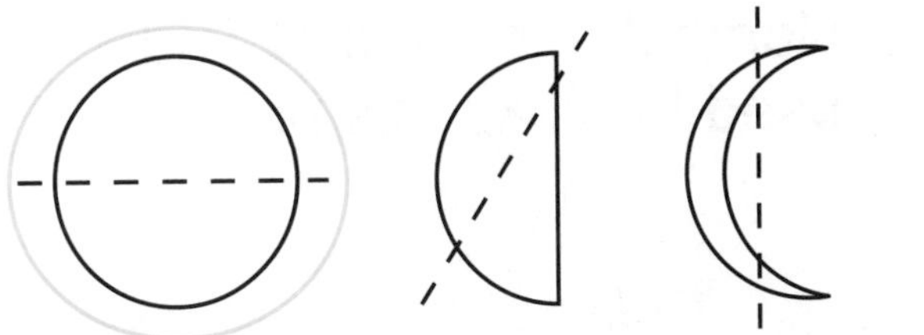

2. Kerri drew a rocket with a line of symmetry. Which rocket did she draw?

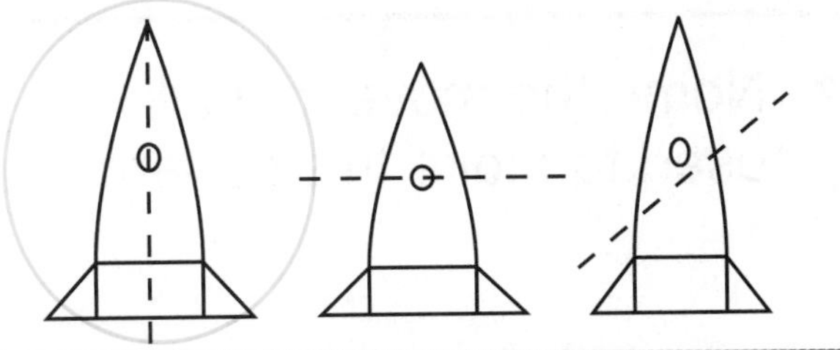

3. Alice drew a number with a line of symmetry. Which number did she draw?

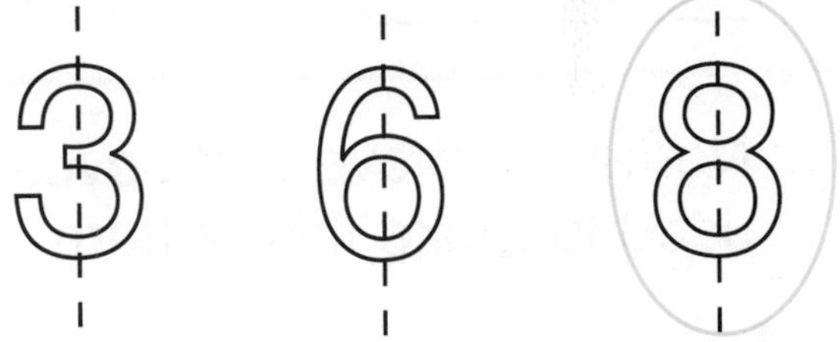

4. Albert drew a jar with a line of symmetry. Which jar did he draw?

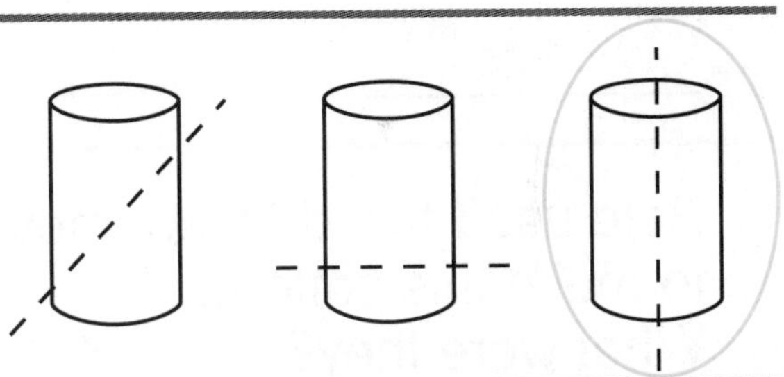

Mark the correct answer.

5. Which letter has a line of symmetry?

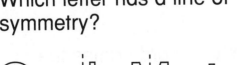

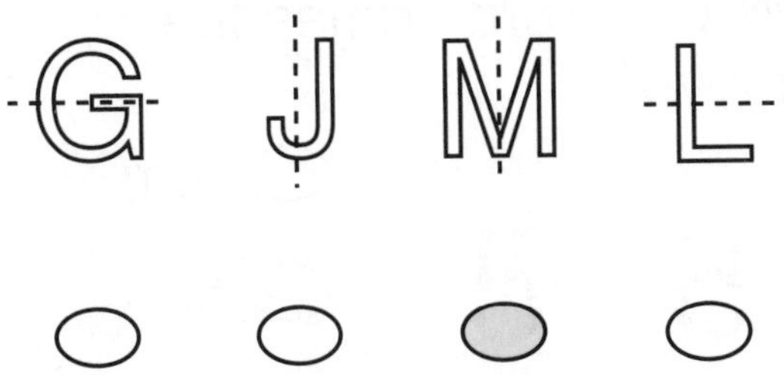

6. Which picture has a line of symmetry?

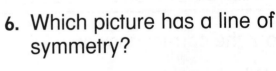

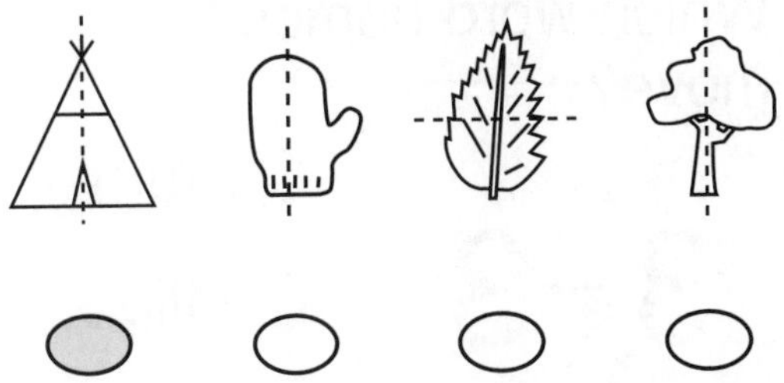

Name ________________________________ **LESSON 20.3**

Understand **Plan** **Solve** **Check**

Slides, Flips, and Turns

Solve.

1. Name the move that Ted used to make this pattern.

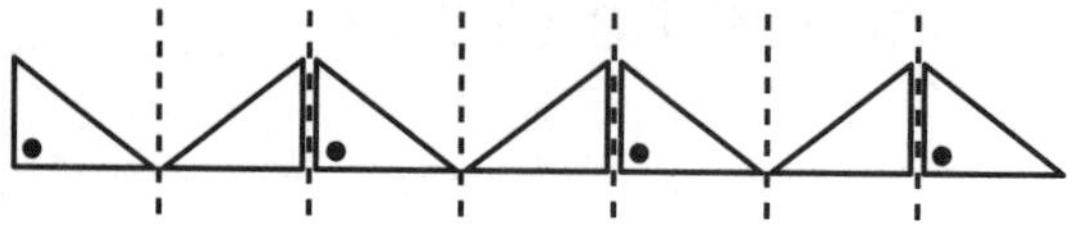

flip

2. Name the move that Jill used to make this pattern.

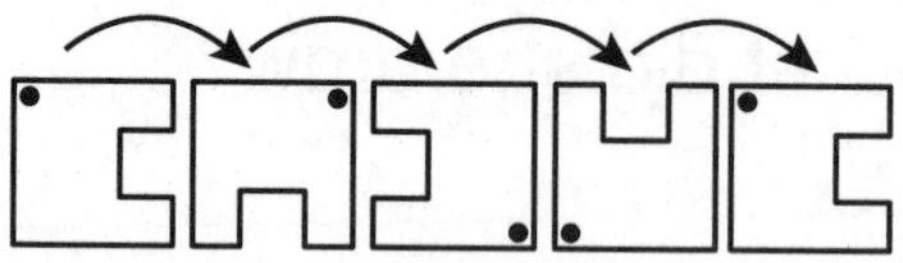

turn

3. Name the move that Joyce used to make this pattern.

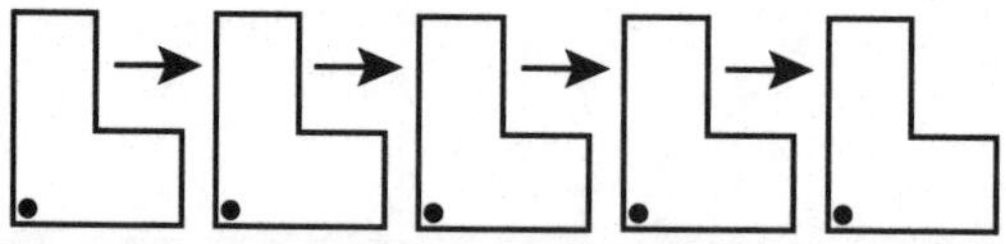

slide

4. Pete used two different moves to make this pattern. What were they?

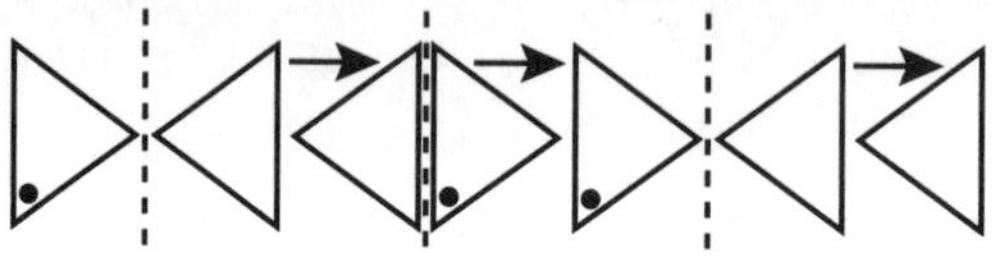

flip and slide

Mark the correct answer.

5. Which word names the move?

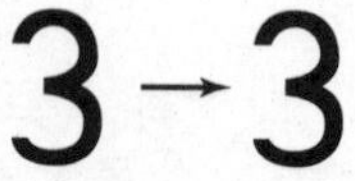

- ○ turn
- ○ flip
- ● slide

6. Which word names the move?

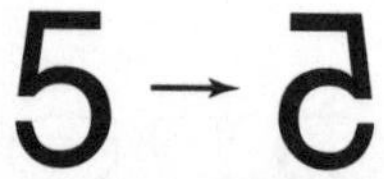

- ○ turn
- ● flip
- ○ slide

Name ______________________________

Reading Strategy: Make a Prediction

Sometimes you can make a prediction based on what you already know.

Jenna predicts that this figure has a line of symmetry. Is Jenna's prediction correct?

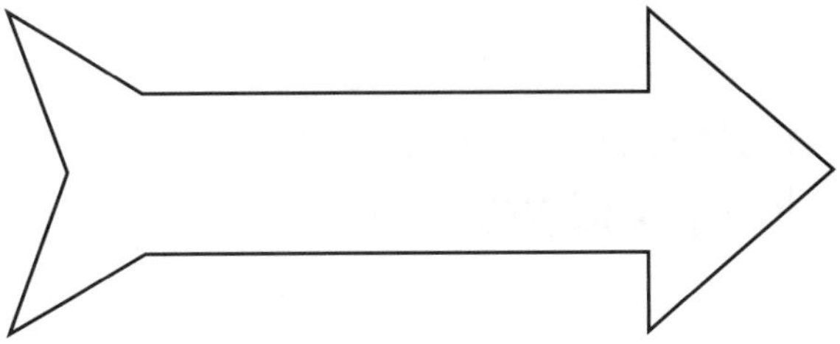

Can you divide the figure into two congruent figures? Draw a line to find out.

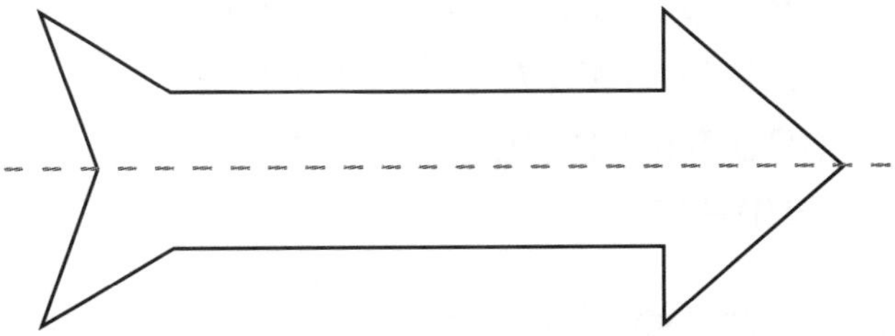

The figure has a line of symmetry. Jenna's prediction is correct.

Make a prediction. Then draw the line of symmetry if that is what you predicted.

1. Does this figure have a line of symmetry? Circle your prediction.
   Prediction: yes no

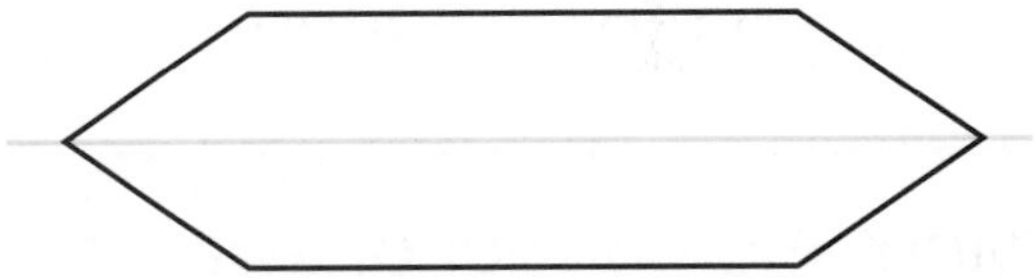

---

2. Does this figure have a line of symmetry? Circle your prediction.
   Prediction: yes no

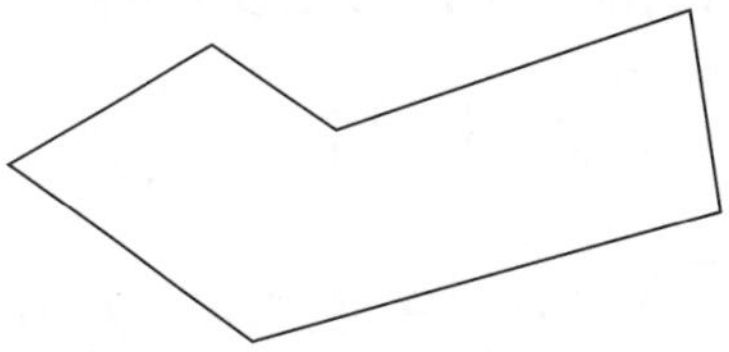

---

3. Does this figure have a line of symmetry? Circle your prediction.
   Prediction: yes no

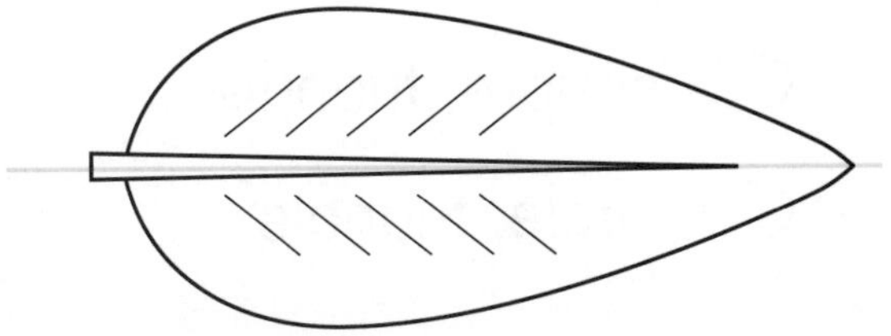

Name ____________________

LESSON 21.1

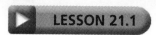

Understand Plan Solve Check

Algebra: Describe Patterns

Draw lines to match the pattern to the snake.
Circle the pattern unit on each snake.

1. Artie saw a snake with a pattern of wide stripes, dots, and wavy lines.

2. Maria watched a snake slither away. It had wide and thin stripes for a pattern.

3. Terry saw a snake with a pattern of thin stripes, wavy lines, and diamonds.

4. A snake crawled under a rock. It had three dots, wide stripes, and thin stripes for a pattern.

A.

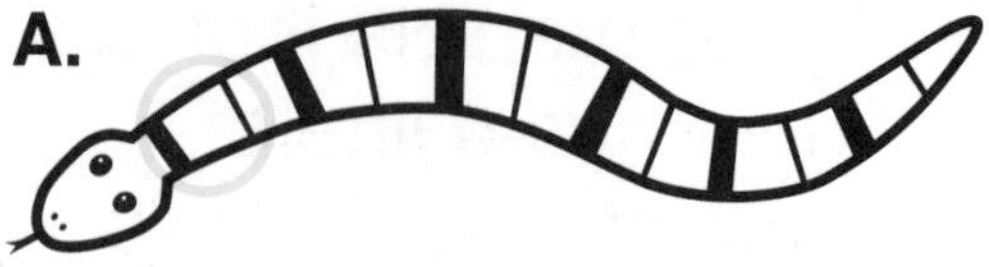

B.

C.

D.

Mark the correct answer.

5. What is the pattern unit?

○ □ △ ○ □ △ ○ □ △

- circle, square, triangle
- circle, triangle, square
- square, triangle
- circle, triangle

6. What is the pattern unit?

— ∼ — ∼ — ∼

- wavy line, dot
- straight line, diamond
- wavy line, straight line, dot
- straight line, wavy line

Name ______________________________

LESSON 21.2

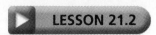

Understand Plan Solve Check

Algebra: Extend Pattern Units

Use your crayon.
Follow the directions.

Check children's work.

1. Color the first square red. Color the second square yellow. Color the third square blue. Repeat the pattern.

R	Y	B	R	Y	B	R	Y	B

2. Color the third square blue. Color the first square green. Color the second square purple. Repeat to extend the pattern.

G	P	B	G	P	B	G	P	B

3. Color the fourth circle red. Color the second circle green. Color the first circle orange. Color the third circle yellow. Repeat to extend the pattern.

O	G	Y	R	O	G	Y	R	O	G	Y	R

Mark the correct answer.

4. What is the pattern unit?

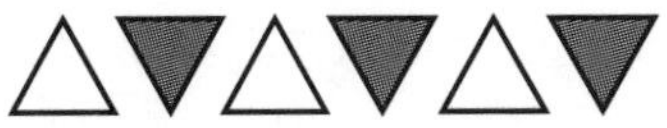

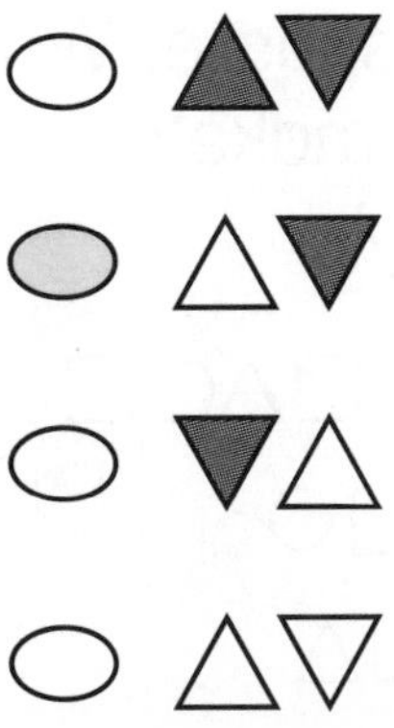

5. What is the pattern unit?

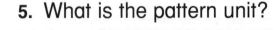

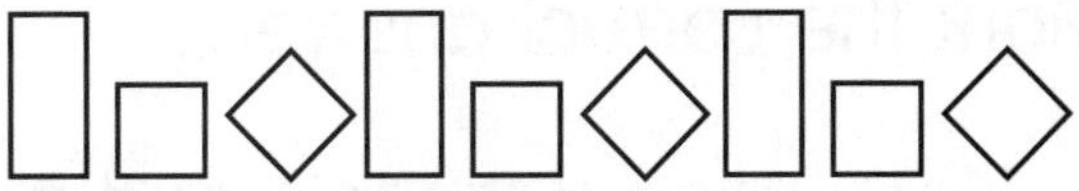

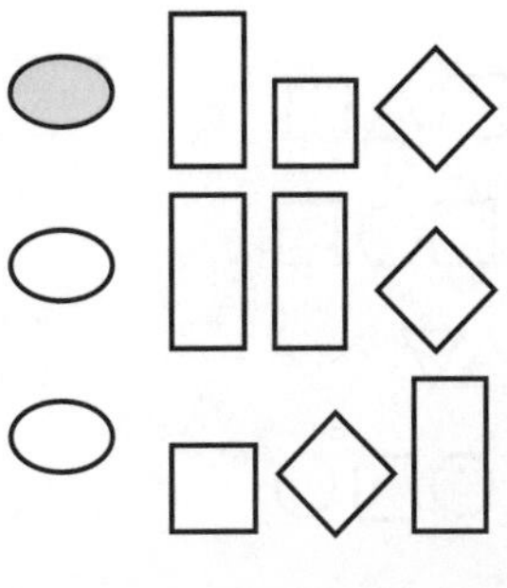

Understand Plan Solve Check

Algebra: Make Patterns

Make the pattern. Circle the pattern unit.

Answers will vary. Possible answers given.

1. James made a pattern unit.
   He used a square and a circle.
   What pattern could he make?

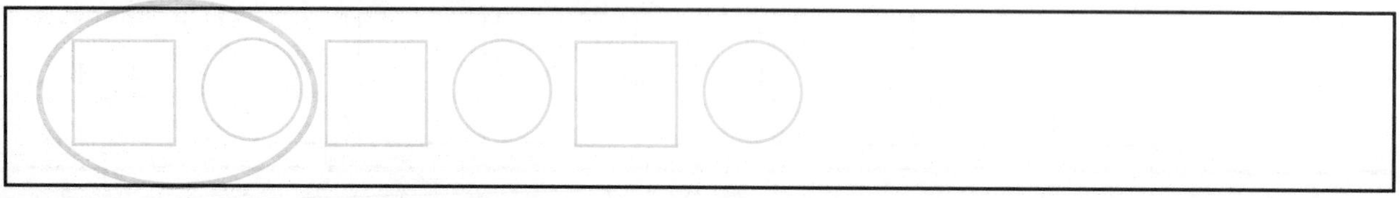

2. Tina made a pattern unit.
   She used a blue circle, a red circle, and a yellow circle.
   What pattern could she make?

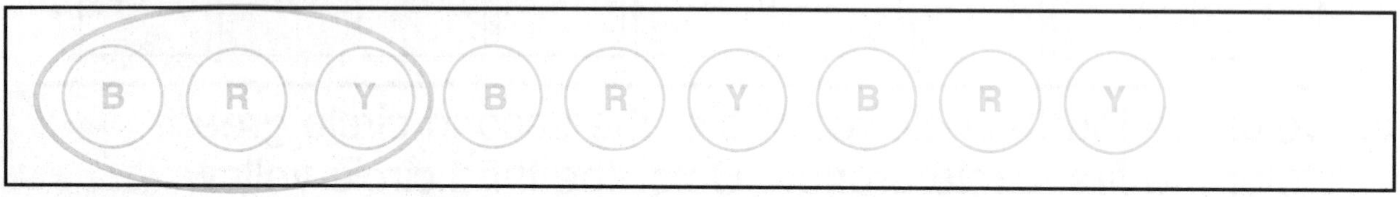

3. Mario made a pattern unit.
   He used a blue square, a circle, and a yellow square.
   What pattern could he make?

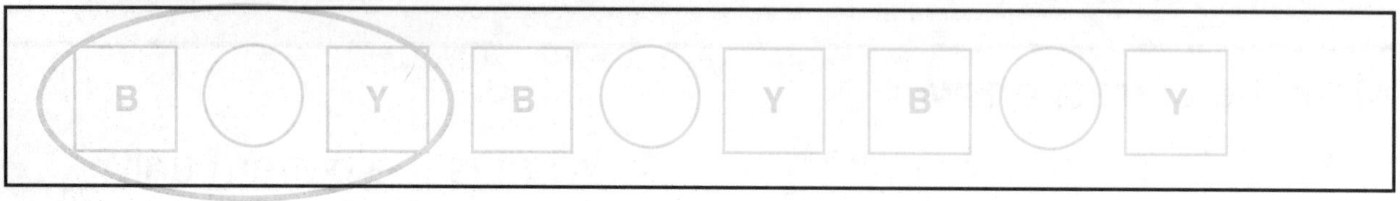

Mark the correct answer.

4. Tony used a triangle and a square. Which pattern did he make?

   ● △□△□△□
   ○ ○□○□○□
   ○ △▽△▽△▽
   ○ □○□○□○

5. Rachel used a circle, a triangle, and a square. Which pattern did she make?

   ○ ○△○△○△
   ● △○□△○□△○□
   ○ □○□○□○
   ○ □△□△□△

Name ______________________________

Reading Strategy: Make a Prediction

Sometimes you need to make a prediction in order to solve a problem. Use what you know to make your prediction.

Mario made this pattern with shapes. Predict which shape he will draw next.

1. What pattern unit did Mario use? 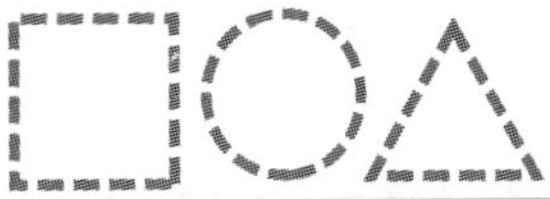 ______________

2. What part of the pattern unit is missing at the end of Mario's pattern?  ______________

3. Predict what the next shape will be.  ______________

Predict what comes next.

4. Predict the next shape in this pattern.

Pattern unit ______________

Prediction ______________

---

5. Predict the next two shapes in this pattern.

Pattern unit ______________

Prediction ______________

Name ________________________________

Understand Plan Solve Check

Reading Strategy • Create Mental Images

Sometimes you can create a picture in your mind to help you solve problems.

Jake made this pattern. He made a mistake. Find the mistake Jake made and correct it.

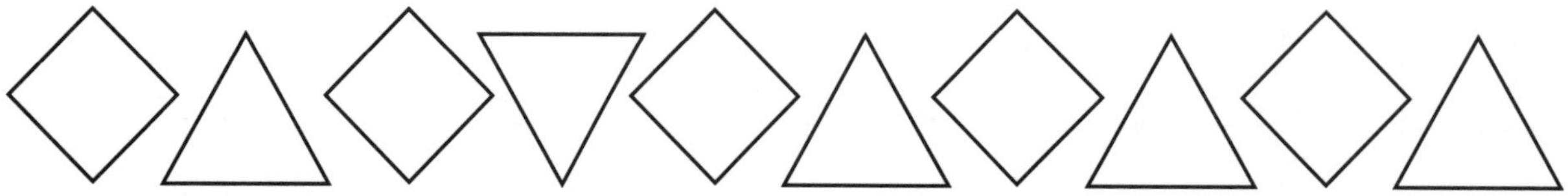

Picture the pattern unit.

Keep the pattern unit in mind. Look for the mistake in the pattern.

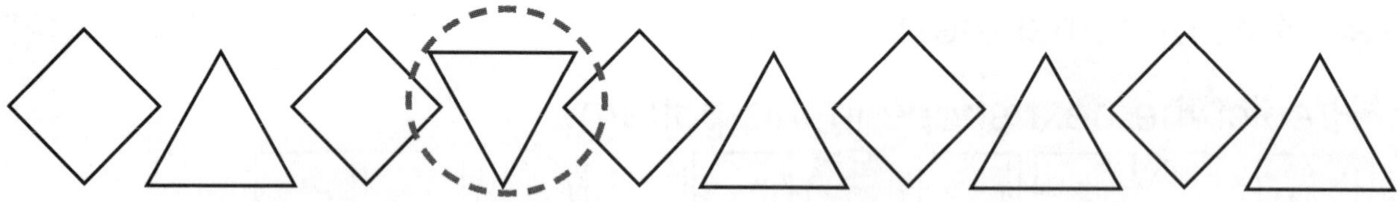

Correct the mistake. 

Picture the pattern unit in your mind. Circle the mistake and correct it.

1.

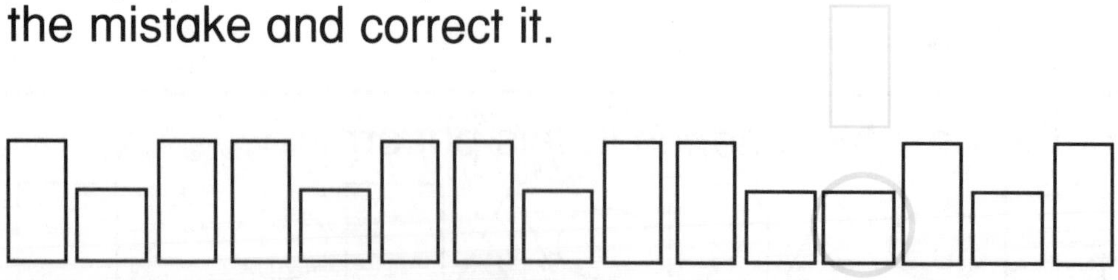

---

2. 1 3 9 1 3 3 1 3 9 1 3 9

9

Name ______________________________

Understand Plan Solve Check

Measure Length with Nonstandard Units

Measure with the given unit.

Answers will vary. Check children's work.

1. About how far is it from your desk to the  ? Measure in footsteps.

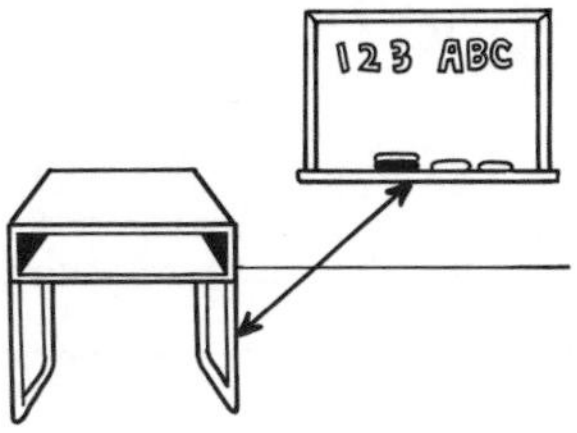

about __________ footsteps

2. About how wide is your chair? Measure in paper clips.

about __________ paper clips

3. About how long is the . Measure in bags.

about __________ bags

4. About how high is your math book? Measure in paper clips.

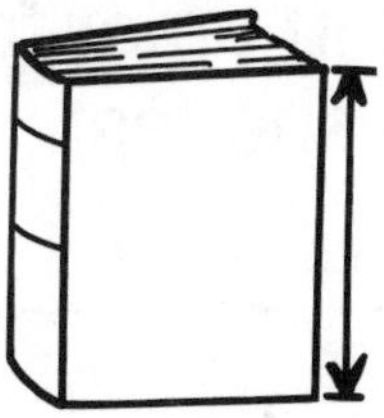

about __________ paper clips

Mark the correct answer.

5. About how many paper clips long is the ribbon?

- ○ about 1 paper clip
- ● about 2 paper clips
- ○ about 3 paper clips
- ○ about 4 paper clips

6. About how many paper clips long is the string?

- ○ about 1 paper clip
- ○ about 2 paper clips
- ● about 3 paper clips
- ○ about 4 paper clips

Name ______________________

Understand Plan Solve Check

Length and Distance

Solve.

1. Mary has a toy dog 6 paper clips tall. Jared has a toy dog 8 paper clips tall. Who has the taller dog?

Jared

2. Mark built a road 14 blocks long. Brad built a road 24 blocks long. Who built the longer road?

Brad

3. Anita made three beaded necklaces using the same size beads. The necklaces have 12 beads, 24 beads, and 18 beads. Put the necklaces in order from longest to shortest.

24 beads
18 beads
12 beads

4. Ryan made three towers using the same size blocks. The towers are 18 blocks tall, 9 blocks tall, and 12 blocks tall. Put the towers in order from shortest to tallest.

9 blocks
12 blocks
18 blocks

Mark the correct answer.

5. About how many paper clips long is the ribbon?

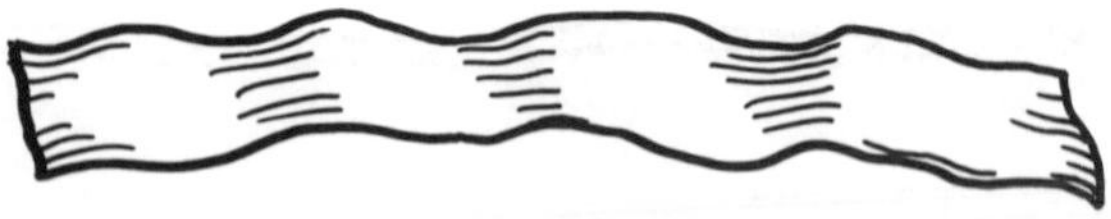

- about 1 paper clip
- about 2 paper clips
- about 3 paper clips
- about 4 paper clips

6. About how many paper clips long is the string?

- about 1 paper clip
- about 2 paper clips
- about 3 paper clips
- about 4 paper clips

Name ______________________________

Understand Plan Solve Check

Measure to the Nearest Inch

Measure to the nearest inch.

Answers will vary. Check children's work.

1. Greg has a paintbrush. He knows it is more than 6 inches long. About how long is a paintbrush?

about ________ inches

2. Karen has a snap cube. She knows it is less than six inches long. About how many inches long is a snap cube?

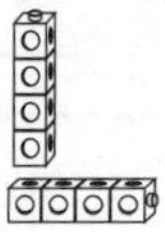

about ________ inches

3. Rosa uses an inch ruler to measure the length of her shoe. About how many inches long is a shoe?

about ________ inches

4. Len has a marker. He used an inch ruler to measure how long it is. About how many inches long is a marker?

about ________ inches

Mark the correct answer.

5. Think about the real object. About how long is it?

- about 1 inch
- about 2 inches
- about 5 inches
- about 12 inches

6. Think about the real object. About how long is it?

- about 20 inches
- about 18 inches
- about 12 inches
- about 6 inches

Name ______________________________

Understand Plan Solve Check

Inch, Foot, and Yard

Think about real objects. Write inches, feet, or yards.

1. Mark measures the length of the canoe.

It is 4 yards long.

2. Kelli measures the length of her whistle.

It is 2 inches long.

3. Bill measures the width of his sleeping bag.

It is 2 feet wide.

4. Stacy measures the highest part of the tent.

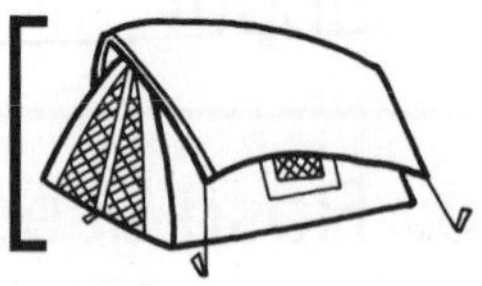

It is 6 feet high.

5. Terri measures her hot dog.

It is 4 inches long.

6. Tim measures a strawberry.

It is 1 inch long.

Mark the correct answer.

7. Which is the best estimate for the real object?

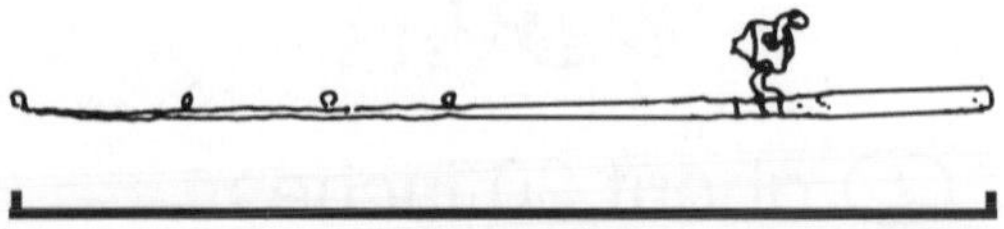

- ○ 6 inches
- ● 2 yards
- ○ 3 inches
- ○ 1 foot

8. Which is the best estimate for the real object?

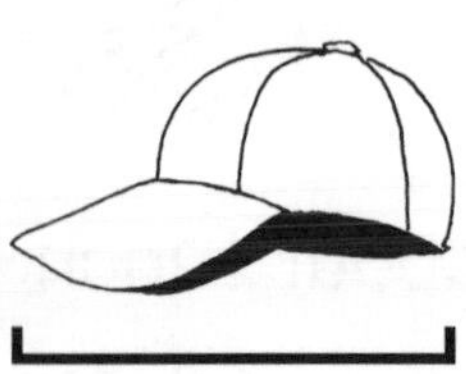

- ○ 3 feet
- ○ 2 yards
- ● 8 inches
- ○ 8 feet

Name ______________________________

Understand Plan Solve Check

Fahrenheit Thermometer

1. How many degrees warmer was it at 2 o'clock?

8 o'clock **2 o'clock**

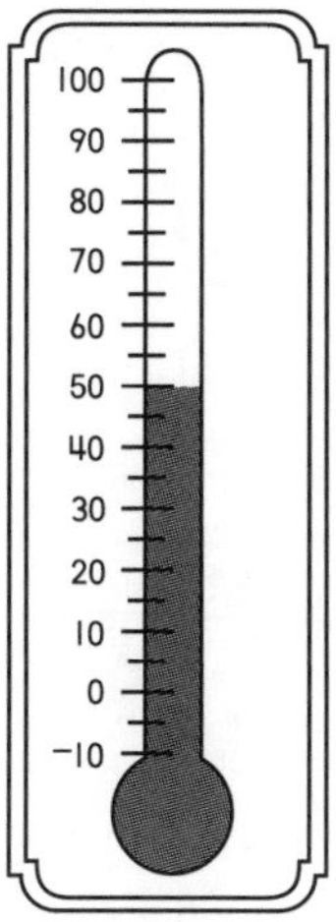

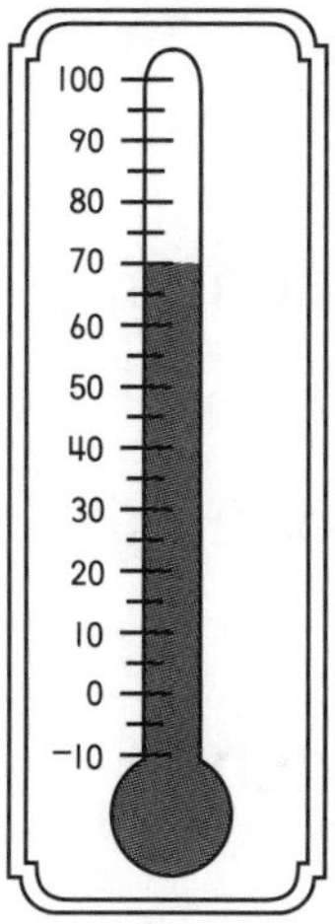

_70_ °F − _50_ °F = _20_ °F

2. The thermometer shows the temperature outside. The temperature inside is 10° warmer. What is the temperature inside?

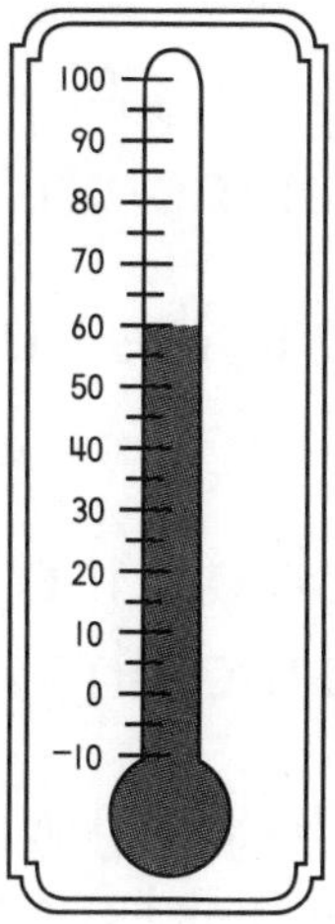

_60_ °F + _10_ °F = _70_ °F

Mark the correct answer.

3. What is the temperature?

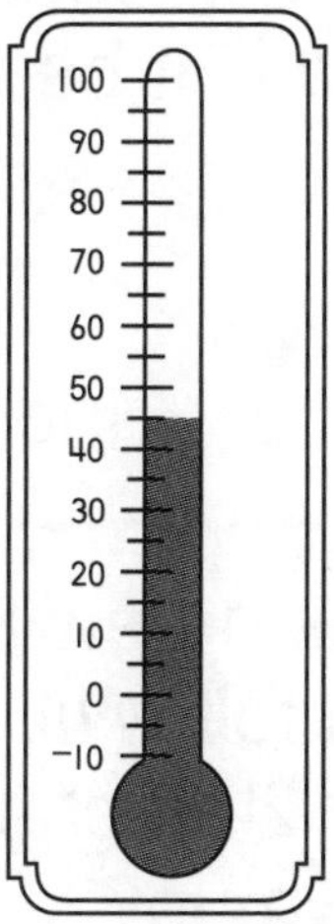

- ○ 40°F
- ○ 41°F
- ● 45°F
- ○ 55°F

4. What is the temperature?

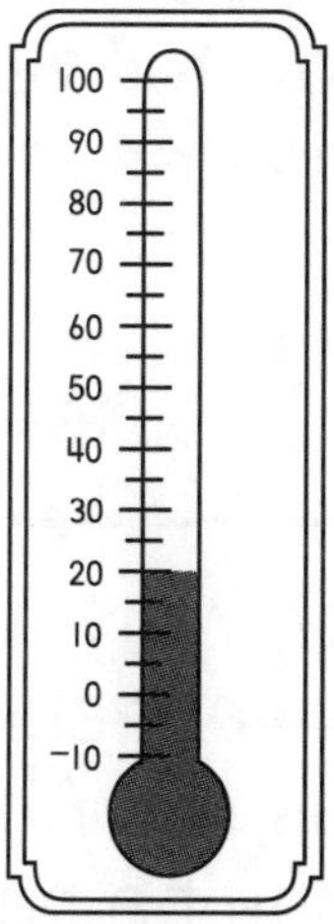

- ○ 10°F
- ● 20°F
- ○ 25°F
- ○ 30°F

Name ______________________________ LESSON 22.6

Understand Plan Solve Check

Reading Strategy • Make Predictions

Sometimes a problem will ask you to find out what happens next.

Alan's puppy is 15 inches long.
Last month it was 12 inches long.
About how long will it be next month?

How long was Alan's puppy last month? __12__ inches

How long is the puppy this month? __15__ inches

How much did the puppy grow in a month? __3__ inches

About how long will the puppy be next month? __15__ + __3__ = __18__ inches

Solve to find out what happens next.

1. Chan planted a tree. This year the tree is 6 feet tall. Last year it was 4 feet tall. About how tall will the tree be next year?

   about __8__ feet tall

2. Ben's tomato plant is 18 inches tall. Last week it was 14 inches tall. About how tall will it be next week?

   about __22__ inches tall

3. This year Patty is 43 inches tall. Last year she was 40 inches tall. About how tall will she be next year?

   about __46__ inches tall

4. Celia has a new kitten. It is 5 inches tall. Will it be about 5, 12, or 24 inches tall when it is grown up?

   about __12__ inches tall

Name ______________________________

Understand Plan Solve Check

Measure Capacity with Nonstandard Units

Solve.

1. Julia fills a mug with water.
Barry fills a wading pool with water.
Who uses more water?

Barry

---

2. Tami makes a pitcher of lemonade.
Angie make a glass of lemonade.
Who makes more lemonade?

Tami

---

3. Lee has a pail full of water.
Craig has a pitcher full of water.
Does Lee or Craig have more water?

Lee

---

4. Pablo fills a bowl with soup.
His sister fills a cup with soup.
Does the cup or the bowl hold more soup?

bowl

Mark the correct answer.

5. Which holds more?

○ 

● 

6. Which holds less?

● 

○ 

Name ______________________

Understand Plan Solve Check

Cups, Pints, Quarts, and Gallons

Solve.

1. Abby bought 2 quarts of juice. Sandy bought 3 pints of juice. Who bought more juice?

   Abby

2. Jean drank 3 cups of water. Carl drank 1 pint of water. Who drank more water?

   Jean

3. Rory bought 3 pints of milk. Antoine bought 1 gallon of milk. Who bought more milk?

   Antoine

4. Louis drank 5 cups of juice. Amy drank 1 quart of juice. Who drank more juice?

   Louis

Mark the correct answer.

5. How many quarts equal 1 gallon?
   - ○ 1 quart
   - ○ 2 quarts
   - ● 4 quarts
   - ○ 8 quarts

6. How many cups equal 3 pints?
   - ○ 2 cups
   - ○ 3 cups
   - ● 6 cups
   - ○ 9 cups

Name ________________

Understand Plan Solve Check

Measure Weight with Nonstandard Units

Solve.

1. Kate wants to know if the disk or the shoe is heavier. She puts them on a scale. Does the shoe side or the disk side dip lower?

shoe side

2. Hanna found a postcard and a golf ball. She used paper clips to weigh them. Did it take more paper clips to weigh the postcard or the golf ball?

golf ball

3. Luis has a sandwich and a cracker for lunch. He put them on a scale to see which was the heaviest. Did the sandwich side or the cracker side dip lower?

sandwich side

Mark the correct answer.

4. Juan put a baseball and a marble on a scale. Which was on the lower side?

- ● baseball
- ○ marble

5. Bella put an apple and a grape on a scale. Which was on the lower side?

- ● apple
- ○ grape

Name ______________________

LESSON 23.4

Understand Plan Solve Check

Ounces and Pounds

Solve.

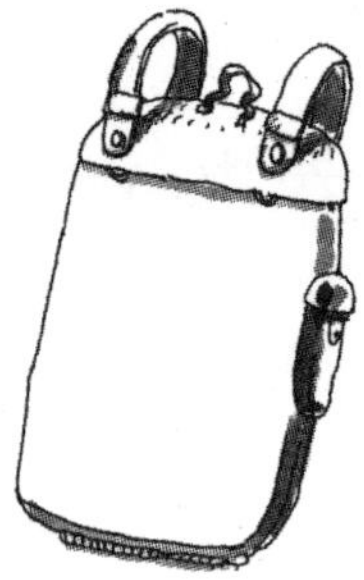

1. Mei's math book is 1 pound.
Her reading book is 2 pounds.
How many pounds of books are in her backpack?

__3__ pounds

2. Tyrell has a 5-pound cat.
Jamal has an 8-pound cat.
How many pounds do their cats weigh together?

__13__ pounds

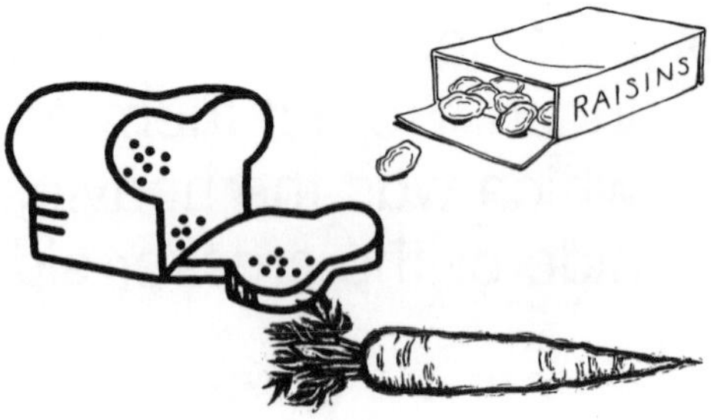

3. The bread needs 3 ounces of raisins.
It needs 8 ounces of carrots.
How many ounces will be added?

__11__ ounces

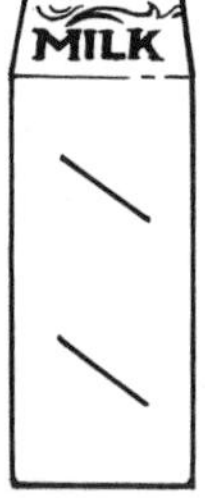

4. Alex drinks 8 ounces of milk for breakfast.
He drinks 8 ounces of milk for dinner.
How many ounces of milk does he drink?

__16__ ounces

Mark the correct answer.

5. Amy wants to know about how heavy a suitcase is.

- ○ about 5 ounces
- ● about 5 pounds

Name ____

LESSON 23.5

Understand Plan Solve Check

Reading Strategy • Use Picture Clues

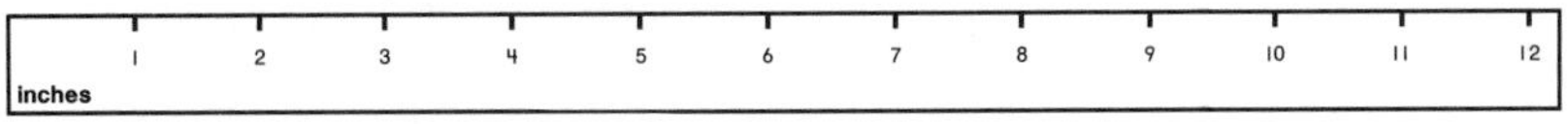

ruler

scale

cup

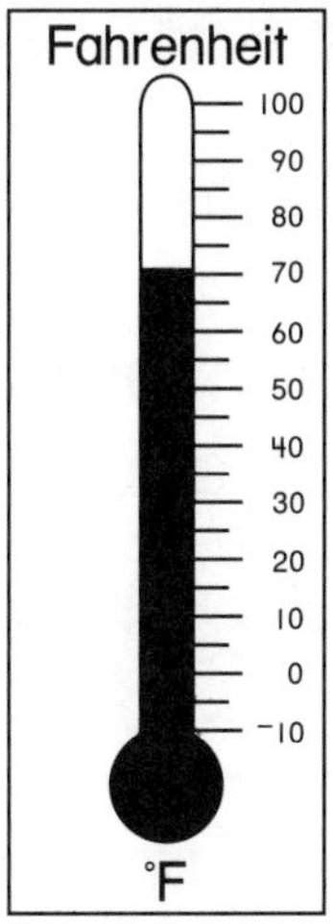

thermometer

Use picture clues to solve.
Write the name of the tool you would use.

1. to find out the temperature on a snowy day.

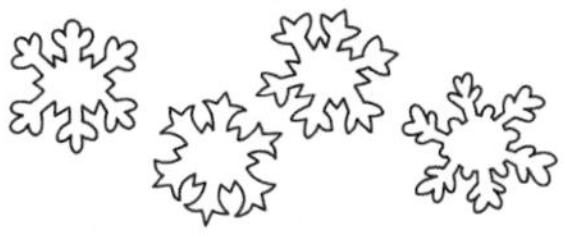

thermometer

2. to find out how much water will fill a bowl.

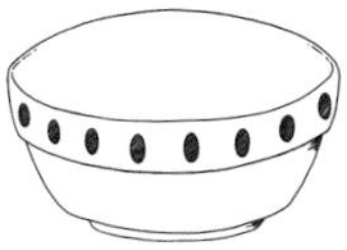

cup

3. to find out the mass of a backpack.

scale

4. to find out how long your pencil is.

ruler

5. to find out the temperature in the freezer.

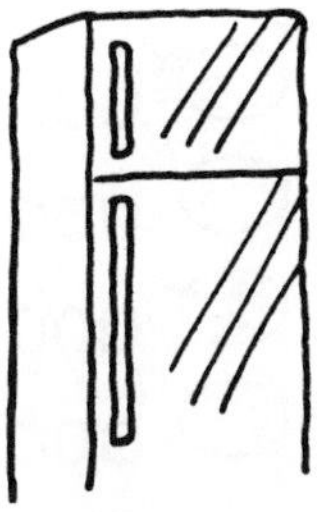

thermometer

Name ______________________

Understand Plan Solve Check

Centimeters and Meters

Think about the real objects. Circle the best answer.

1. Jennifer measures the toaster.
   It is about

   16 centimeters   16 meters   high.

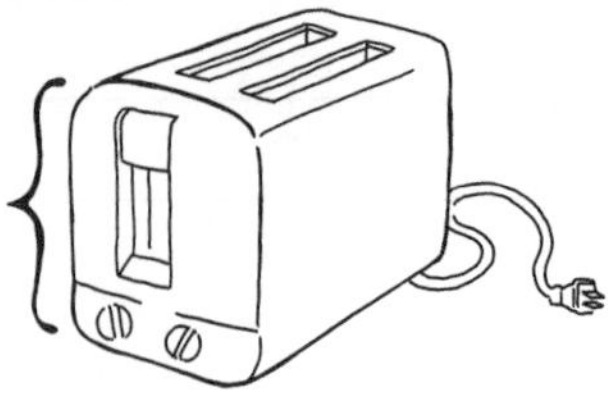

2. Mimi measures the table.
   It is about

   3 centimeters   3 meters   long.

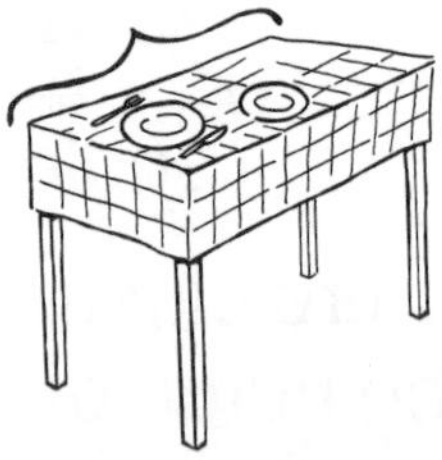

3. Dan measures a cereal box.
   It is about

   25 centimeters   25 meters   high.

4. Dan measures the refrigerator.
   It is about

   2 centimeters   2 meters   high.

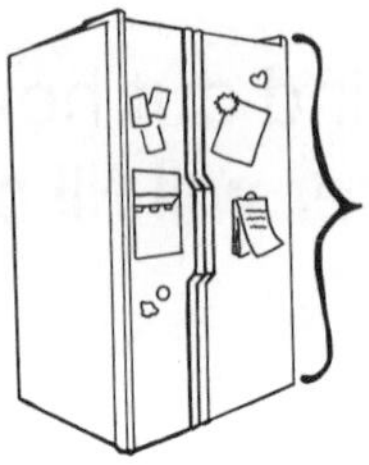

Mark the best answer.

5. About how long is a slice of bacon?

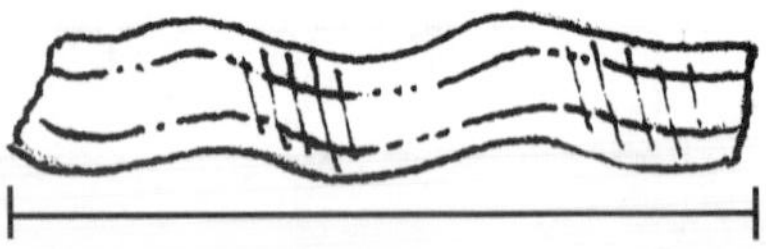

- about 18 centimeters
- about 18 meters
- about 1 centimeter
- about 1 meter

6. About how tall is a milk carton?

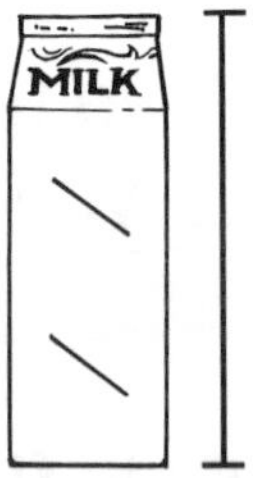

- about 3 centimeters
- about 3 meters
- about 24 centimeters
- about 24 meters

Name ____________________

LESSON 24.2

Understand Plan Solve Check

Milliliters and Liters

Solve.

1. Liz says a drop of water is about 1 milliliter. Dan says it is about 1 liter. Who is right?

   Liz

2. Peter has a fish tank. He wants to know how much it holds. Will Peter use milliliters or liters to find out?

   liters

3. Mr. Chin is getting gas for his car. Does the gas tank hold about 60 milliliters or about 60 liters?

   about 60 liters

4. Raul is taking a spoonful of peanut butter. Does the spoon hold milliliters or liters?

   milliliters

5. Mira wants to fill a watering can with water. Will she need about 4 milliliters or about 4 liters to fill the can?

   about 4 liters

6. Kyle wants to measure the amount of orange juice in a pitcher. Will he measure the juice in liters or milliliters?

   liters

Mark the correct answer.

7. About how much will an eyedropper hold?

- ● about 10 milliliters
- ○ about 1 liter
- ○ more than 1 liter

8. How much water will it take to fill a wading pool?

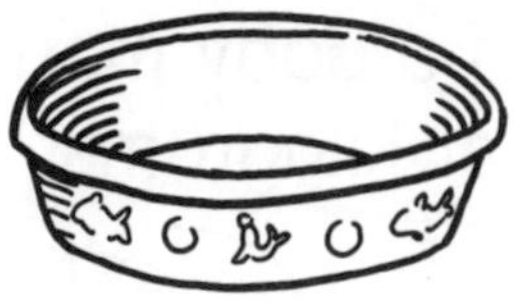

- ○ about 10 milliliters
- ○ about 1 liter
- ● more than 1 liter

Name ______________________________

Understand Plan Solve Check

Grams and Kilograms

Circle the better answer.

1. An adult cat has a mass of about 6 kilograms. What might be the mass of a kitten?

16 kilograms

850 grams

2. A baby elephant has a mass of about 2,000 kilograms. What might be the mass of an adult elephant?

2,000 kilograms

5,000 kilograms

3. A lamb has a mass of about 50 kilograms. What might be the mass of an adult sheep?

150 kilograms

900 kilograms

4. An adult rabbit has a mass of about 1 kilogram. What might be the mass of a baby rabbit?

1 kilogram

100 grams

Mark the correct answer.

5. Would you measure the mass of a baby mouse in grams or kilograms?

○ grams

○ kilograms

6. Would you measure the mass of a human baby in grams or kilograms?

○ grams

○ kilograms

Name ______________________

LESSON 24.4

Understand Plan Solve Check

Celsius Thermometer

1. Rico looks out the window. It is a cold, rainy day. Rico checks the thermometer. Is the temperature 5°C or 25°C?

5°C

2. Ruby says it is a good day for building a snowman. She looks at the thermometer. Is the temperature 0°C or 38°C?

0°C

3. Luisa and her friends are going outside to the pool. Luisa checks the temperature. is the temperature 0°C or 32°C?

32°C

4. Jody is going for a walk. His mother says it is 34°C outside. Will Jody wear a coat or a T-shirt?

T-shirt

5. Martha says that 40°C is a very hot day. Tony says it is a cold day. Who is right?

Martha

6. The thermometer shows 18°C. Steve wants to round the temperature to the nearest ten degrees. What does he say the temperature is?

20°C

Mark the correct answer.

7. What temperature is it?

○ 10°C
○ 15°C
● 18°C
○ 22°C

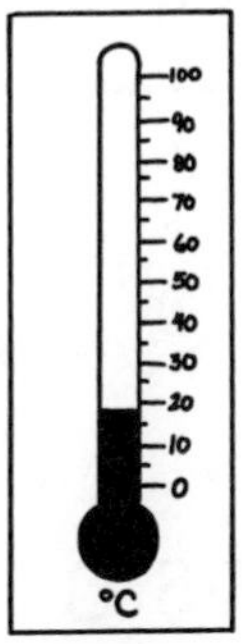

8. What temperature is it?

○ 17°C
○ 24°C
○ 30°C
● 33°C

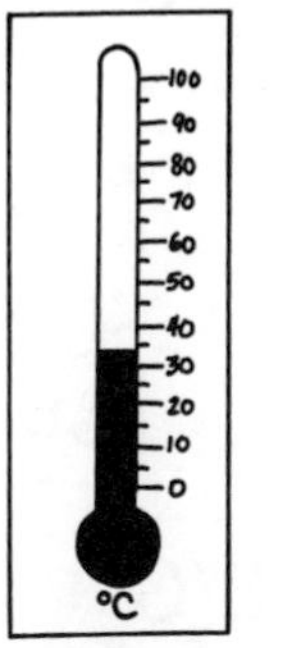

Name ______________________________

LESSON 24.5

Understand Plan Solve Check

Reading Strategy • Use Picture Clues

Using pictures can help you solve problems.

The children are playing outside.
Rosa looks at the thermometer.
Is the temperature 0°C or 33°C?

Look at the picture for clues.

What is the weather like? snowing

What are the children wearing? coats

What are the children doing? making a snowman

Solve the problem.
The temperature is 0°C.

Look for picture clues.
Then circle the better estimate.

1. 

18°C (32°C)

2. 

30°C (2°C)

3. 

(28°C) 5°C

4. 

(45°C) 20°C

Name ______________________

Understand Plan Solve Check

Perimeter

Solve.

1. Sue drew a square. Each side of the square was 4 centimeters long. What was the perimeter of the square Sue drew?

16 centimeters

2. Fred drew a triangle. Two of the sides were 5 centimeters long. One side was 3 centimeters long. What was the perimeter of Fred's triangle?

13 centimeters

3. Dante drew a rectangle. Two of the sides were 7 centimeters long. Two of the sides were 2 centimeters long. What was the perimeter of Dante's rectangle?

18 centimeters

4. Tina has a garden. Each of the 4 sides is 12 feet long. Tina wants to put a fence around the garden. How much fence will she need?

48 feet

5. Cole's room is shaped like a rectangle. Two sides are 12 feet long. Two sides are 10 feet long. What is the perimeter of Cole's room?

44 feet

6. Kimi cut a triangle from a piece of paper. Each side of the triangle was 5 inches long. What was the perimeter of Kimi's triangle?

15 inches

Mark the correct answer.

7. The side of a square is 3 feet. What is the perimeter?

- ○ 8 feet
- ● 12 feet
- ○ 16 feet
- ○ 20 feet

8. One side of a triangle is 2 feet. Two sides are 4 feet. What is the perimeter of the triangle?

- ○ 2 feet
- ○ 8 feet
- ● 10 feet
- ○ 12 feet

Name ______________________

LESSON 25.2

Understand Plan Solve Check

Area

Solve.

Check children's coloring.

1. Marc and Janna each drew a figure. Find the area of each figure. Color the one that has more units.

Marc

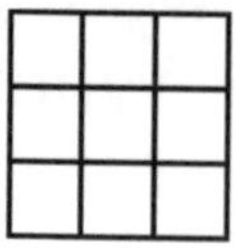

Janna

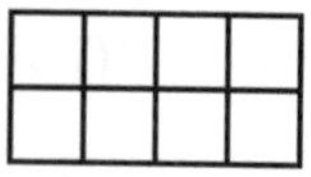

9 units   8 units

2. Jeff and Casey each drew a figure. Find the area of each figure. Color the one that has more units.

Jeff

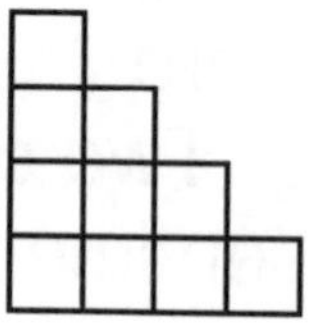

Casey

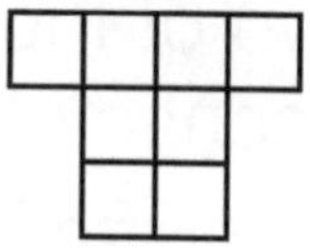

10 units   8 units

3. Amy and Tani each drew a figure. Find the area of each figure. Color the one that has more units.

Amy

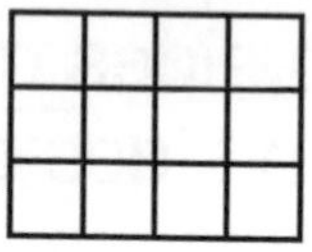

Tani

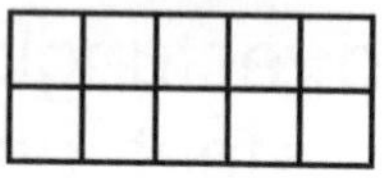

12 units   10 units

Find the area.
Mark the correct answer.

4.

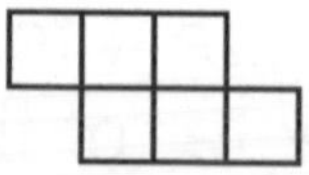

- ○ 8 units
- ● 6 units
- ○ 4 units
- ○ 2 units

5.

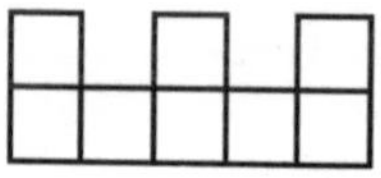

- ● 8 units
- ○ 6 units
- ○ 4 units
- ○ 2 units

Name ______________________________

Understand Plan Solve Check

Reading Strategy • Make Predictions

Kishi wants to know the perimeter of her table. She measures each side. Two sides are 4 feet long. Two sides are 2 feet long. What will Kishi do next to find the perimeter?

add the measurements

What is the perimeter of the table? 10 feet

Decide what will happen next. Then solve.

1. Ryan wants to know the perimeter of his room. The room is a square. Ryan measures one side. It is 10 feet long. What does he do next?

   adds 10 four times

   What is the perimeter of Ryan's room?

   40 feet

2. Tony wants to find the area of his desk. He covers the desk with tiles. What does Tony do next to find the area of his desk?

   counts the tiles

   Tony uses 18 tiles. What is the area of his desk?

   18 units

3. Mika wants to know the perimeter of her garden. She measures each side. Two sides are 10 feet long. Two sides are 8 feet long. What does Mika do next?

   adds the measurements

   What is the perimeter of Mika's garden?

   24 units

4. Dixie is making a gift for a friend. She wants to know how many tiles she needs to cover it. First she predicts how many. Then what does she do?

   checks

   Dixie uses 24 tiles. How much area does she cover?

   36 feet

Name ______________________________

LESSON 25.4

Understand Plan Solve Check

Volume

Solve.

1. Mark has a shoe box. 12 cubes cover the bottom. The box can fit 4 layers of cubes. What is the volume of Mark's shoe box?

   48 cubes

2. April has a box. There are 8 cubes in the bottom layer of the box. The box can fit 2 layers of cubes. What is the volume of the box?

   16 cubes

3. Paul makes a solid figure with cubes. First he makes a row of 3 cubes. Then he puts 3 rows of cubes together. What is the volume of the solid figure Paul makes?

   9 cubes

4. Derek makes a row of 5 cubes. Then he puts another row of 5 cubes on top. What is the volume of the solid figure Derek makes?

   10 cubes

5. Judy makes a tower of cubes. The tower is 4 layers high. Each layer has 6 cubes. What is the volume of the tower Judy makes?

   24 cubes

6. Len wants to find the volume of a container. He covers the bottom with 5 cubes. It takes 5 layers to fill the container. What is the volume?

   25 cubes

Find the volume. Mark the correct answer.

7. 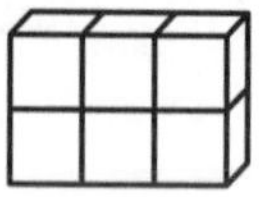

   ○ 3 cubes ○ 5 cubes
   ○ 4 cubes ● 6 cubes

8. 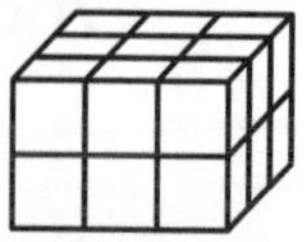

   ○ 6 cubes ● 18 cubes
   ○ 12 cubes ○ 20 cubes

Name ______________________________

Understand | Plan | Solve | Check

Unit Fractions

Solve. Write the fraction.

1. Mark divided a square into 4 equal parts. Then he painted one of the parts. How much of the square did Mark paint?

   $\frac{1}{4}$ of the square

2. Anna cut a pizza into 5 equal pieces. Then she gave one of the pieces to Rosa. How much of the pizza did Anna give to Rosa?

   $\frac{1}{5}$ of the pizza

3. Juan divided a sandwich into 2 equal parts. Then he ate one of the parts. How much of the sandwich did Juan eat?

   $\frac{1}{2}$ of the sandwich

4. Chet divided a circle into 8 equal parts. Then he shaded one of the parts. How much of the circle did Chet shade?

   $\frac{1}{8}$ of the circle

Mark the correct answer.

5. What is the fraction for the shaded part?

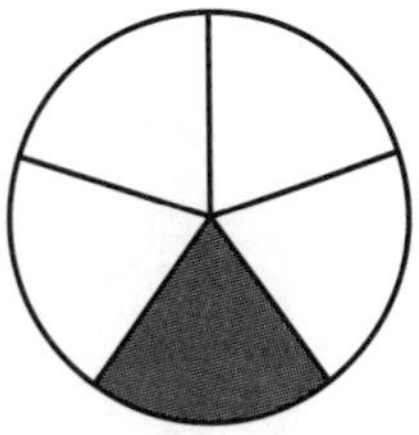

○ $\frac{1}{3}$ ● $\frac{1}{5}$

○ $\frac{1}{4}$ ○ $\frac{1}{6}$

6. What is the fraction for the shaded part?

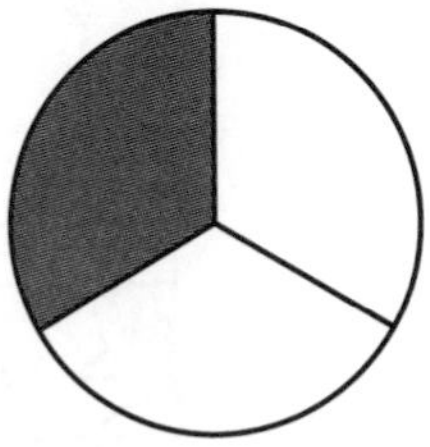

○ $\frac{1}{2}$ ○ $\frac{1}{4}$

● $\frac{1}{3}$ ○ $\frac{1}{6}$

Name ____________________

Understand Plan Solve Check

Reading Strategy • Use Picture Clues

Sometimes picture clues can help you solve a problem.

Kita has 2 rice cakes to share. She gives $\frac{1}{2}$ of a rice cake to Kyle. She gives $\frac{1}{3}$ of a rice cake to Ellen. Who has the larger piece?

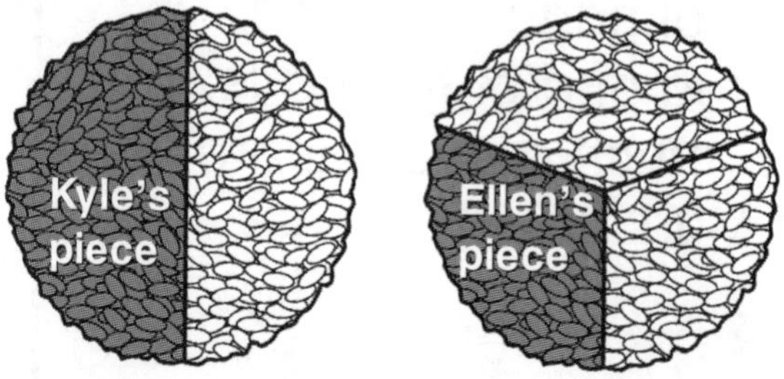

Use the pictures to solve.

Who has the larger piece of rice cake? Kyle

Use the picture clues to help you solve the problem.

1. Adam has 2 burritos to share. He gives Mari $\frac{1}{4}$ of a burrito. He gives Luis $\frac{1}{5}$ of a burrito. Who has the larger piece?

Mari

2. Litsa has 2 corn cakes to share. She gives $\frac{1}{3}$ of a corn cake to Debbie. She gives $\frac{1}{6}$ of a corn cake to Darren. Who has the larger piece?

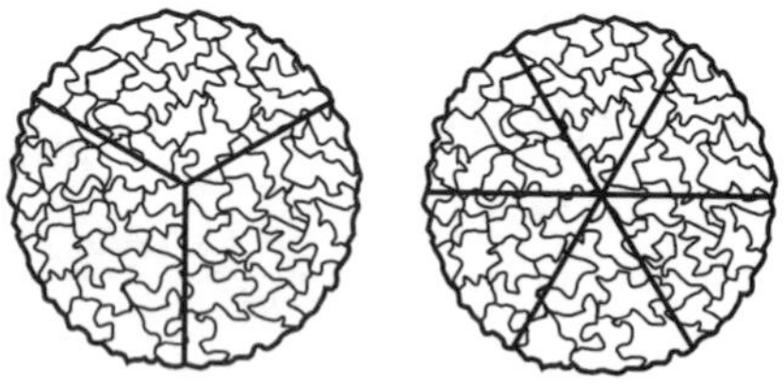

Debbie

Name ______________________________

Understand | Plan | Solve | Check

Other Fractions

Color to show the fraction. Check children's coloring.

1. Amy makes a flag that is $\frac{1}{2}$ red and $\frac{1}{2}$ blue.

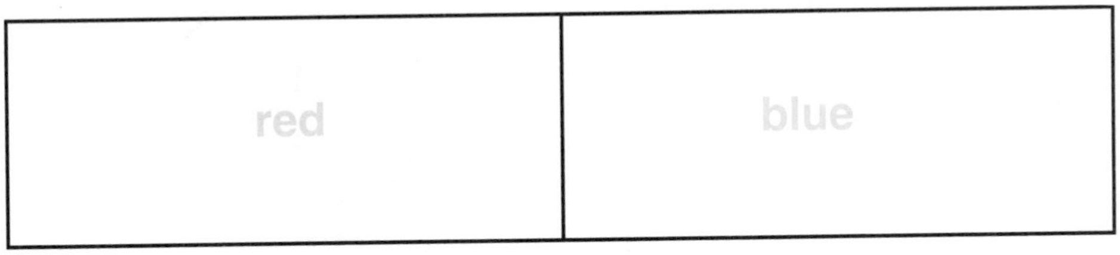

2. Irene makes a flag that is $\frac{1}{4}$ green and $\frac{3}{4}$ yellow.

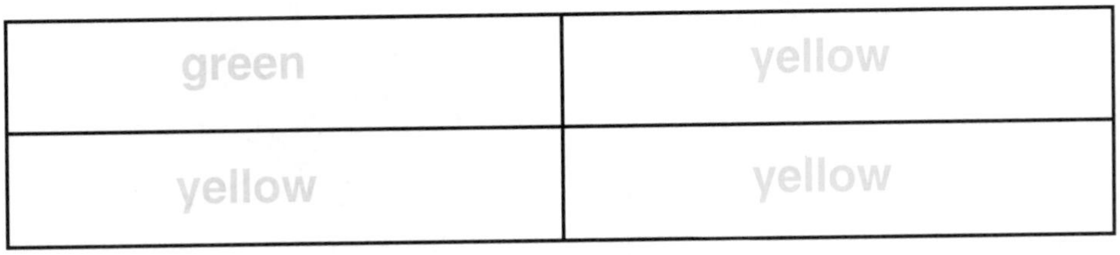

3. Todd makes a flag that is $\frac{1}{3}$ red and $\frac{2}{3}$ yellow.

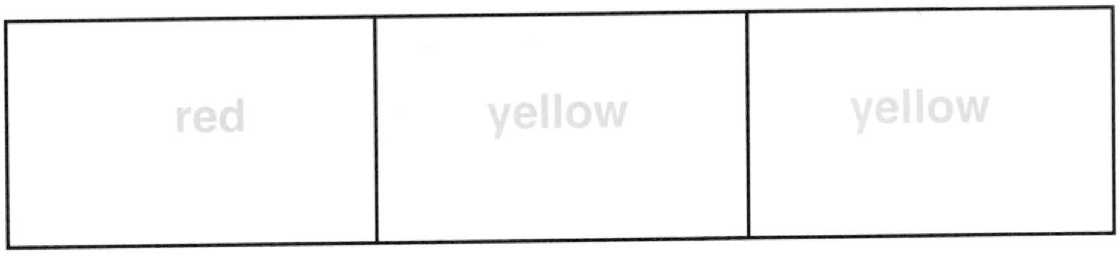

Mark the correct answer.

4. Which fraction matches the picture?

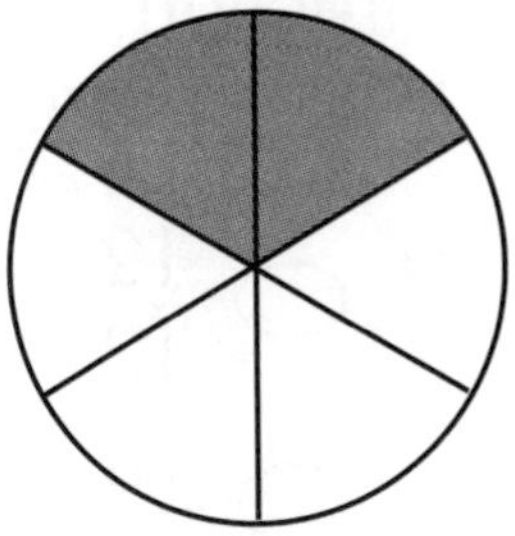

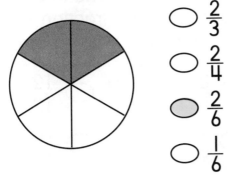

- ○ $\frac{2}{3}$
- ○ $\frac{2}{4}$
- ● $\frac{2}{6}$
- ○ $\frac{1}{6}$

5. Which fraction matches the picture?

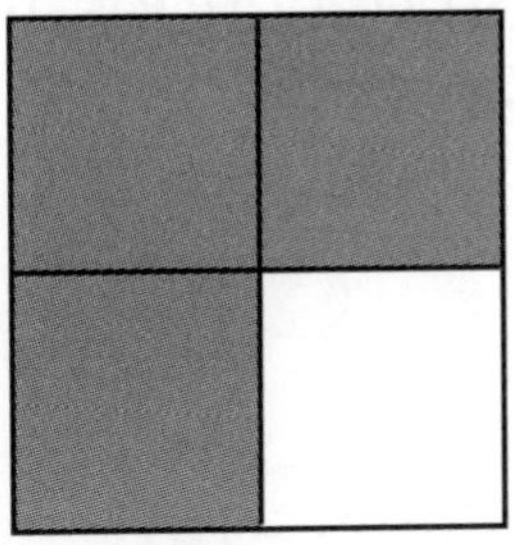

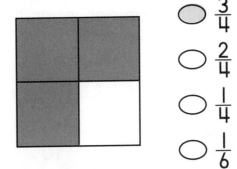

- ● $\frac{3}{4}$
- ○ $\frac{2}{4}$
- ○ $\frac{1}{4}$
- ○ $\frac{1}{6}$

Name ______________________________ LESSON 26.4

Understand Plan Solve Check

Fractions Equal to 1

Color to show the whole.
Write the fraction that equals the whole. Check children's work.

1. Nora cuts a pie into 4 parts. Each piece is $\frac{1}{4}$.

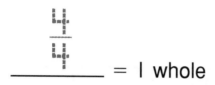

$\frac{4}{4}$ = 1 whole

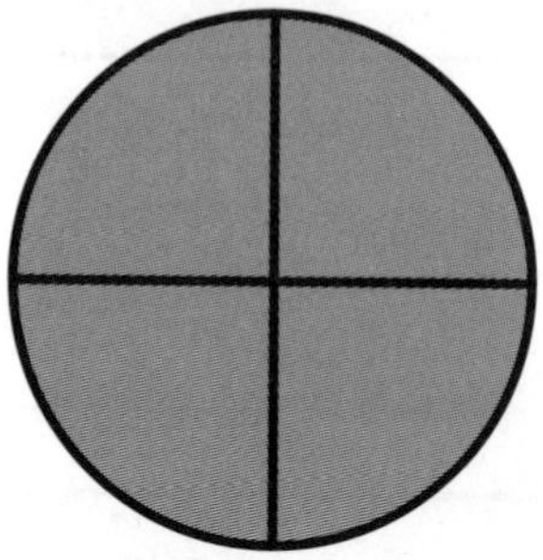

2. Rosa cuts a pizza into 16 parts. Each piece is $\frac{1}{16}$.

$\frac{16}{16}$ = 1 whole

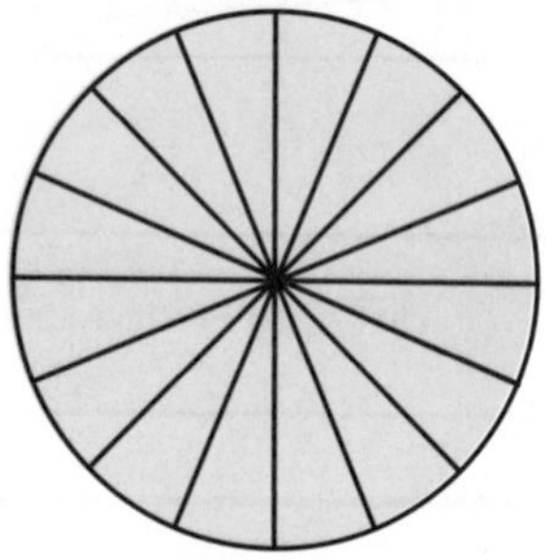

3. Simon cuts a pizza into 5 parts. Each piece is $\frac{1}{5}$.

$\frac{5}{5}$ = 1 whole

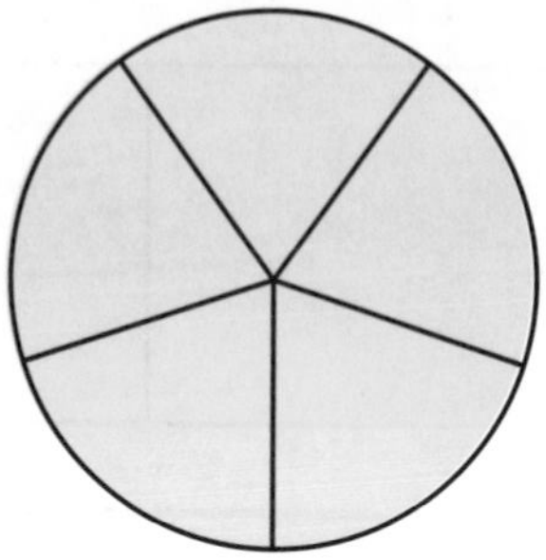

Mark the correct answer.

4. Rick cuts a pizza into 7 parts. Which fraction describes the whole pizza?

○ $\frac{5}{5}$ ● $\frac{7}{7}$

○ $\frac{8}{8}$ ○ $\frac{10}{10}$

5. Eileen cuts a pizza into 8 parts. Which fraction describes the whole pizza?

● $\frac{8}{8}$ ○ $\frac{12}{12}$

○ $\frac{9}{9}$ ○ $\frac{16}{16}$

Name ______________________

Understand Plan Solve Check

Unit Fractions of a Group

Solve. Write the fraction.

1. There are 6 pizzas at the party. One pizza is sausage. What fraction of the pizzas is the sausage pizza?

   $\frac{1}{6}$ of the pizzas

2. There are 12 different drinks at the party. One drink is lemonade. What fraction of the drinks is the lemonade?

   $\frac{1}{12}$ of the drinks

3. There are 15 chairs at the party. One chair is empty. What fraction of the chairs is the empty chair?

   $\frac{1}{15}$ of the chairs

4. There are 7 video games at the party. One game is broken. What fraction of the games is the broken game?

   $\frac{1}{7}$ of the games

5. There are 5 banners at the party. One of the banners is blue. What fraction of the banners is the blue banner?

   $\frac{1}{5}$ of the banners

6. There are 8 presents at the party. One of the presents is open. What fraction of the presents is the open present?

   $\frac{1}{8}$ of the presents

Mark the correct answer.

7. What fraction is shaded?

- (●) $\frac{1}{4}$
- ( ) $\frac{1}{8}$
- ( ) $\frac{1}{6}$
- ( ) $\frac{1}{10}$

8. What fraction is shaded?

- ( ) $\frac{1}{6}$
- ( ) $\frac{1}{11}$
- (●) $\frac{1}{9}$
- ( ) $\frac{1}{12}$

Understand Plan Solve Check

Other Fractions of a Group

Solve. Write the fraction.

1. Lisa has 3 red flowers. Jackie has 2 yellow flowers. What fraction of the flowers are the yellow flowers?

$\frac{2}{5}$ of the flowers

2. Cory has 4 small toy cars. Robby has 4 big toy cars. What fraction of the toy cars are the small toy cars?

$\frac{4}{8}$ of the toy cars

3. There are 7 dogs. 3 dogs do not have spots. 4 dogs have spots. What fraction of the dogs do **not** have spots?

$\frac{3}{7}$ of the dogs

4. There are 4 children wearing shirts. 1 shirt has stripes. What fraction of the shirts do **not** have stripes?

$\frac{3}{4}$ of the shirts

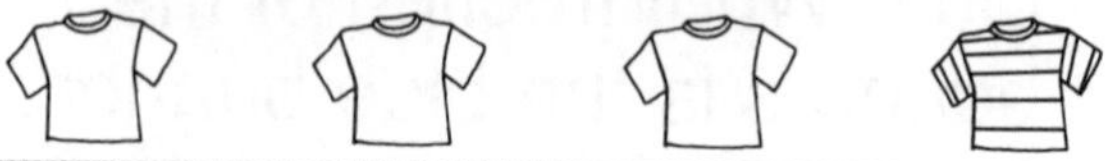

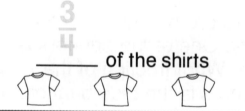

Mark the correct answer.

5. What fraction is shaded?

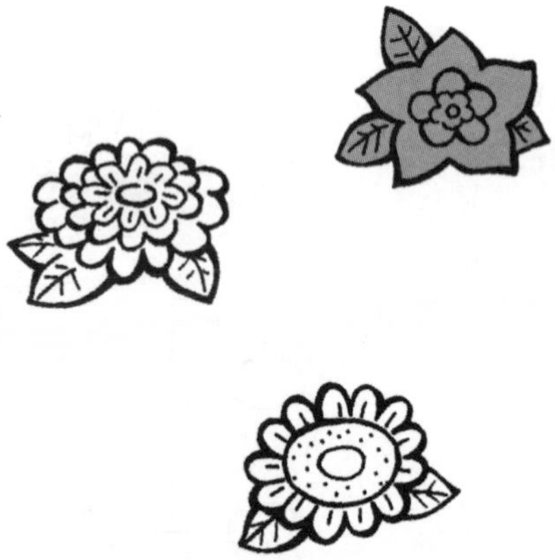

- $\frac{1}{2}$
- $\frac{1}{3}$
- $\frac{2}{6}$
- $\frac{1}{6}$

6. What fraction is white?

- $\frac{1}{8}$
- $\frac{2}{6}$
- $\frac{2}{8}$
- $\frac{6}{8}$

Name ____________________

Understand Plan Solve Check

Hundreds

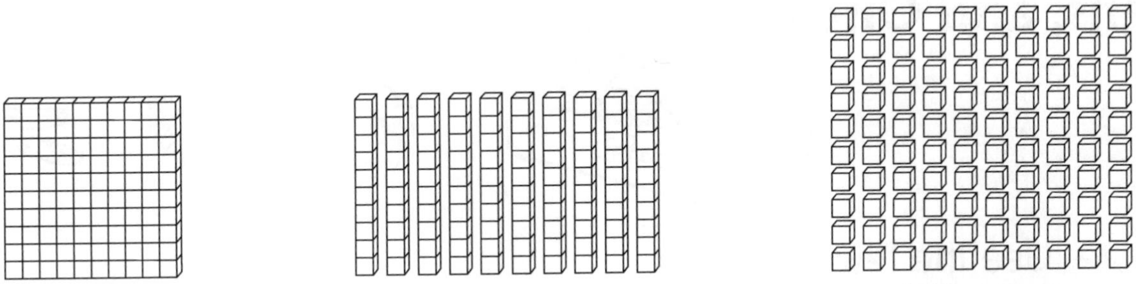

1 hundred = 10 tens = 100 ones

Solve.

1. There are 100 stamps in a sheet. Mr. Vincent buys 900 stamps. How many sheets does he buy?

   9 sheets

2. There are 100 pencils in a box. The principal buys 3 boxes. How many pencils does he buy?

   300 pencils

3. There are 100 sheets in a pack of paper. Beth buys 5 packs. How many sheets of paper does she buy?

   500 sheets of paper

4. There are 100 paper clips in a box. Mr. Davis buys 700 paper clips. How many boxes does he buy?

   7 boxes

Mark the correct answer.

5. How many tens are there?

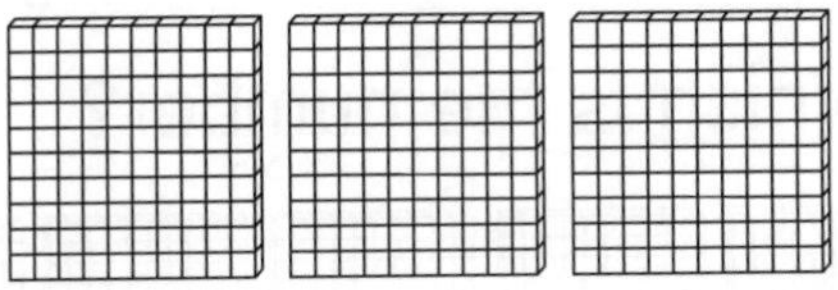

   - ○ 3
   - ● 30
   - ○ 300

6. How many ones are there?

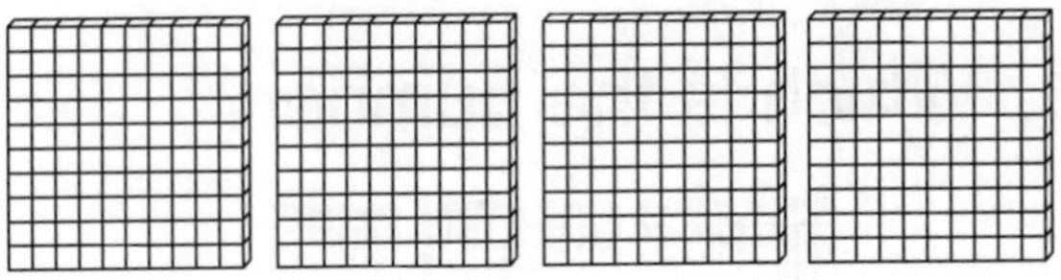

   - ○ 4
   - ○ 40
   - ● 400

Name ______________________________

Understand Plan Solve Check

Hundreds, Tens, and Ones

Solve. Use the fewest boxes.

1. Mr. Morris buys safety pins for 238 people. What does he buy?

   __2__ boxes of 100 __3__ boxes of 10 __8__ single pins

2. Ms. Webster buys 200 safety pins. What does she buy?

   __2__ boxes of 100 __0__ boxes of 10 __0__ single pins

3. A teacher buys 404 safety pins. What does she buy?

   __4__ boxes of 100 __0__ boxes of 10 __4__ single pins

4. A store owner buys 335 safety pins. What does he buy?

   __3__ boxes of 100 __3__ boxes of 10 __5__ single pins

Mark the correct answer.

5. Which is the number?

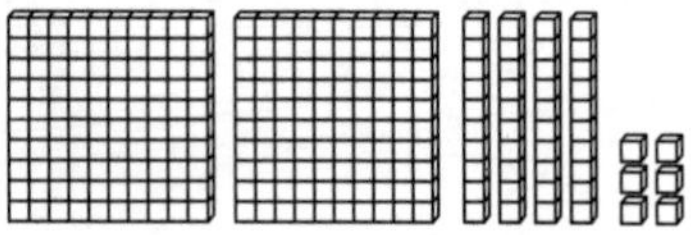

- (●) 246
- ( ) 462
- ( ) 264
- ( ) 426

6. Which is the number?

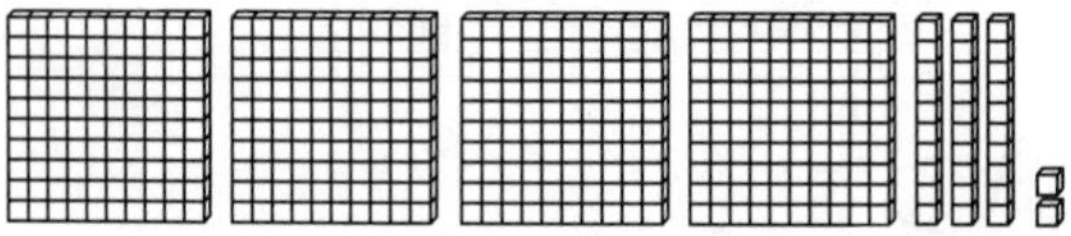

- ( ) 423
- ( ) 324
- (●) 432
- ( ) 342

Name ______________________________

Understand Plan Solve Check

Place Value

Circle the value of the underlined digit.

1. Marty has 6<u>9</u>2 paper clips.

   900 (90) 9

2. Maria has 32<u>7</u> books.

   700 70 (7)

3. Kendra has 87<u>1</u> sheets of paper.

   100 10 (1)

4. Rob has 1<u>3</u>8 staples.

   300 (30) 3

5. Angel has 4<u>6</u>3 pencils.

   600 (60) 6

6. Russell has <u>5</u>89 erasers.

   (500) 50 5

Mark the most reasonable estimate.

7. _____ people live in my house.

   ● 4
   ○ 40
   ○ 400

8. There are _____ children in Miss Smith's class.

   ○ 2
   ● 20
   ○ 200

Name ________________________________

Understand Plan Solve Check

Algebra: Different Ways to Show Numbers

Write the number. Then show it a different way.

1. Ara's number has an 8 in the hundreds place. It has a 3 in the ones place and an 8 in the tens place. What is her number?

hundreds	tens	ones
8	8	3

883

2. Maya's number has a 1 in the tens place. It has a 9 in the ones place and a 2 in the hundreds place. What is her number?

200 + 10 + 9

219

3. Taro's number has a 4 in the tens place. It has a 1 in the hundreds place and a 2 in the ones place. What is his number?

hundreds	tens	ones
1	4	2

142

4. Jina's number has a 4 in the ones place. It has a 3 in the tens place and a 9 in the hundreds place. What is her number?

9 hundreds 3 tens 4 ones

934

Mark the correct answer.

5. six hundred seventy-one

- ○ 176
- ● 671
- ○ 617
- ○ 761

6. $400 + 4$

- ○ 44
- ● 404
- ○ 400
- ○ 444

Name ___________________________

Understand Plan Solve Check

Reading Strategy • Retell the Story

Sometimes retelling a problem in your own words can help you solve it.

Jada's mother gives her a 1 dollar bill, 4 dimes, and 3 pennies. Her father gives her 2 dollar bills, 2 dimes, and 1 penny. How much money does Jada have in all?

Retell the problem.

1. Jada's mother gives her $1.43.

2. Jada's father gives her $2.21.

3. Jada has $3.64 in all.

Retell the problem in your own words. Then solve.

4. Devon has 3 dollar bills and 2 pennies. His sister gives him 4 dimes and 2 pennies. How much money does he have now?

$3.44

5. Ilana's grandfather gives her 1 dime and 7 pennies. Her grandmother gives her 1 dollar bill and 5 dimes. How much money does Ilana have now?

$1.67

Understand Plan Solve Check

Algebra: Compare Numbers: >, <, and =

Write > or < in the circle.
Solve.

1. There are 562 adults and 652 children at the zoo. Are there more adults or children at the zoo?

   $562 \ (<) \ 652$

   children

2. The zoo sold 218 bags of peanuts and 281 bags of popcorn. Were more bags of peanuts or popcorn sold?

   $218 \ (<) \ 281$

   popcorn

3. On Tuesday 716 children visited the park. On Wednesday 709 children visited. On which day did fewer children visit?

   $716 \ (>) \ 709$

   Wednesday

4. There are 462 trees in the town park. There are 284 trees in the city park. Are there fewer trees in the town park or the city park?

   $462 \ (>) \ 284$

   city park

Mark the correct answer.

5. Choose >, <, or =.

   $505 \ \bigcirc \ 505$

   ○ <
   ○ >
   ● =

6. Choose > or <.

   $200 \ \bigcirc \ 20$

   ● >
   ○ <

Name ______________________________

LESSON 28.2

Understand Plan Solve Check

Missing Numbers to 1,000

Use 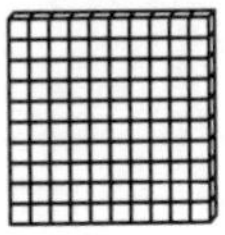, , and to show the numbers.
Write the missing numbers.

1. Tara, Simon, Olivia, and Mark got tickets for a show. The numbers were in order. Mark's ticket was number 342. Olivia's ticket was 344. What were the ticket numbers for Tara and Simon?

341	342	343	344
Tara	Mark	Simon	Olivia

2. Four friends ran in a race. Each person was given a number. Tony's number was 287. Julio's number was 290. What were the numbers for Clark and Kelly?

287	288	289	290
Tony	Clark	Kelly	Julio

3. The Broncos basketball team played four games. At each game they scored one more point than before. The last game's score was 112. What were the scores for the other three games?

109	110	111	112
1	2	3	4

4. Jesse, Amy, Tran, and Jim had seats at a play. Their seat numbers were in order. Jesse's seat was number 594. Tran's seat was number 596. What were the other two seat numbers?

594	595	596	597
Jesse	Amy	Tran	Jim

Mark the correct answer.

5. Which number is missing?
946, 947, ______

- ○ 945
- ○ 949
- ● 948
- ○ 950

6. Which number is missing?
______, 800, 801

- ○ 803
- ● 799
- ○ 802
- ○ 798

Name ____________________

LESSON 28.3

Understand Plan Solve Check

Algebra: Order Numbers on a Number Line

Use the number line to help you.

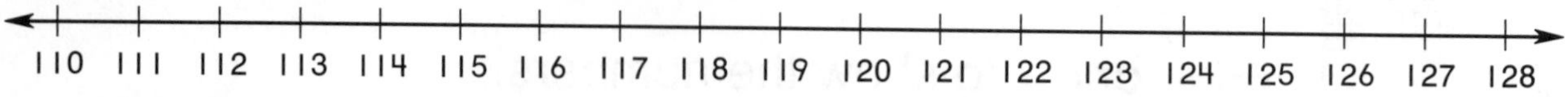

1. Stacey has 113 crayons. Herbie has 111 crayons. Jonah has 126 crayons. Put the numbers of crayons in order from the least to the greatest.

   111 113 126

2. Juan has 128 markers. Sue has 115 markers. Joe has 122 markers. Put the numbers of markers in order from the least to the greatest.

   115 122 128

3. Laurie has 119 stickers. Rochelle has 112 stickers. Sam has 116 stickers. Put the numbers of stickers in order from the least to the greatest.

   112 116 119

4. Joan has 110 paper clips. Pat has 126 paper clips. María has 119 paper clips. Put the numbers of paper clips in order from the least to the greatest.

   110 119 126

5. David has 124 marbles. Ali has 127 marbles. Lynn has 120 marbles. Put the numbers of marbles in order from the least to the greatest.

   120 124 127

6. Emily has 117 nuts. Karen has 127 nuts. Carmen has 121 nuts. Put the numbers of nuts in order from the least to the greatest.

   117 121 127

Mark the correct answer.

7. Which number is the least?

   ○ 120 ○ 126 ● 117

8. Which number is the greatest?

   ○ 123 ● 128 ○ 115

Name ______________________

Understand Plan Solve Check

Algebra: Find Unknown Numbers on a Number Line

Use the clues.
Show the letter on the number line.
Then read across to solve the riddle.

What can speak every language in the world?

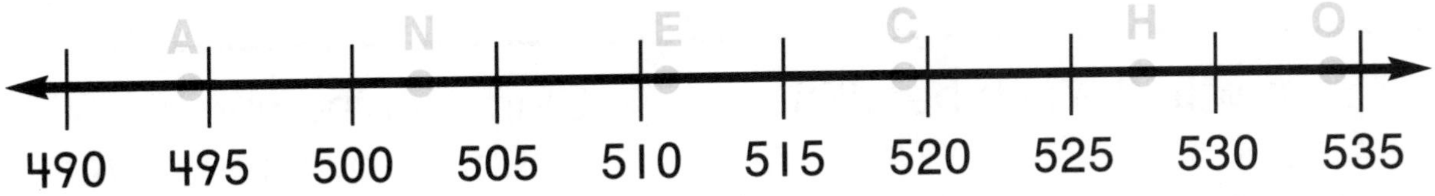

1. My tens digit is 1.
My hundreds digit is 5
My ones digit is 9.
What number am I? 519

Label me **C** on the number line.

2. My hundreds digit is 4.
My ones digit is 4.
My tens digit is 9.
What number am I? 494

Label me **A** on the number line.

3. I am 10 more than 524.
What number am I? 534

Label me **O** on the number line.

4. I am 20 less than 523.
What number am I? 503

Label me **N** on the number line.

5. I am 10 more than 501.
What number am I? 511

Label me **E** on the number line.

6. I am 20 less than 548.
What number am I? 528

Label me **H** on the number line.

Mark the correct answer.

7. What number is at the dot?

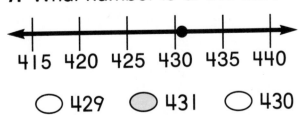

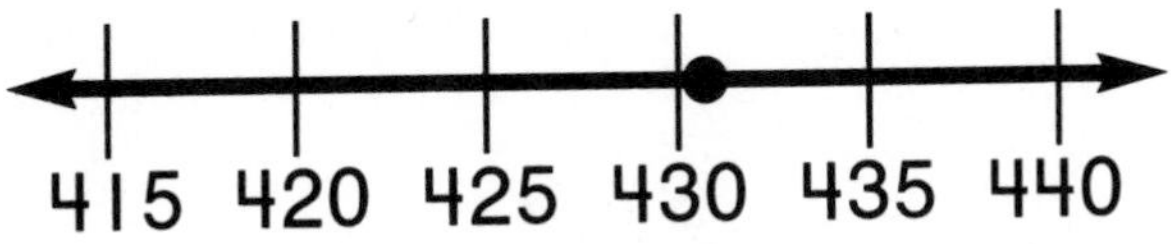

○ 429 ● 431 ○ 430

8. What number is at the dot?

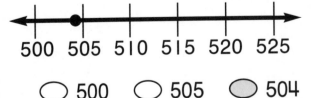

○ 500 ○ 505 ● 504

Name ______________________________

Understand Plan Solve Check

Algebra: Skip-Count

Skip-count. Write the missing numbers.

1. Start with the number 123. Count on by twos. What will the next three numbers be?

   123, 125, 127, 129

2. You count by fives and end with 255. What are the first three numbers?

   240, 245, 250, 255

3. Start with the number 398. Count on by fours. What will the next three numbers be?

   398, 402, 406, 410

4. Start with the number 503. Count on by threes. What will the next three numbers be?

   503, 506, 509, 512

5. You count by tens and end with 895. What are the first three numbers?

   865, 875, 885, 895

6. Count on by fives. Start with the number 612. What will the next three numbers be?

   612, 617, 622, 627

Mark the correct answer.

7. Which number is missing?

   376, 380, _____, 388, 392

   ○ 382 ○ 385
   ● 384 ○ 386

8. Which number is missing?

   997, 995, 993, _____, 989

   ○ 919 ● 991
   ○ 988 ○ 999

Name ____________________

Understand Plan Solve Check

Reading Strategy • Make Predictions

Sometimes a problem asks you to tell what will happen.

Ben wants to be a better swimmer.
On Monday he swims 3 laps.
On Tuesday he swims 6 laps.
On Wednesday he swims 9 laps.
How many laps will Ben likely swim on Thursday?

Look for a pattern.

laps Ben swam on Monday 3

laps Ben swam on Tuesday 6

laps Ben swam on Wednesday 9

What is the pattern? 3 more each time

laps Ben will likely swim on Thursday 12

Solve.

1. Mia is learning to knit. She knits 4 rows the first day. She knits 8 rows the second day. She knits 12 rows the third day. How many rows will Mia likely knit on the fourth day?

16 rows

2. Jeff is starting to lift weights. He lifts 20 pounds the first month. He lifts 30 pounds the second month. He lifts 40 pounds the third month. How many pounds will Jeff likely lift the fourth month?

50 pounds

Name ____________________

Understand Plan Solve Check

Mental Math: Add Hundreds

Use the addition facts you know to help you solve the problem.

1. Randy counts 400 ants on the playground. Then he counts 200 ants by the bus stop. How many ants does he count in all?

   $$\begin{array}{r} 400 \\ +\ 200 \\ \hline 600 \end{array}$$

   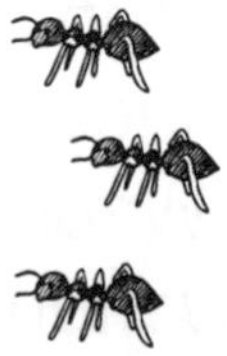

   600 ants

2. Mrs. Brach's room has 300 books. Mr. Corey's room has 500 books. How many books are in both classrooms?

   $$\begin{array}{r} 300 \\ +\ 500 \\ \hline 800 \end{array}$$

   800 books

3. 100 children sing in the school chorus. 200 children listen to the chorus. How many children are there in all?

   $$\begin{array}{r} 100 \\ +\ 200 \\ \hline 300 \end{array}$$

   300 children

Mark the correct answer.

4. Gina's class sells 600 granola bars and 100 bags of peanuts. How many items do they sell in all?

   ○ 300 ● 700
   ○ 500 ○ 900

5. At the soccer game, there are 300 children from Tom's school and 200 children from Tami's school. How many children are at the game in all?

   ○ 300 ● 500
   ○ 400 ○ 600

Name ______________________

LESSON 29.2

Understand Plan Solve Check

Model 3-Digit Addition: Regroup Ones

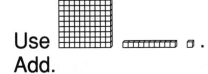

Use 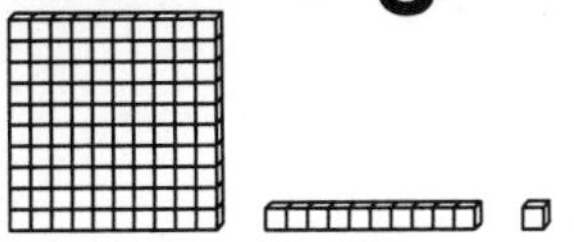 .
Add.

1. Mr. Chen ordered 144 bottles of orange juice and 248 bottles of grape juice for his store. How many bottles of juice did he order?

392 bottles

2. Mr. Cameron ordered 636 stuffed dogs and 227 stuffed cats for his toy store. How many stuffed animals did he order?

863 stuffed animals

3. Mrs. Daily ordered 415 red beads and 239 white beads to make jewelry. How many beads did she order?

654 beads

4. Mr. Hooper ordered 278 roses and 319 daisies for his flower shop. How many flowers did he order?

597 flowers

Mark the correct answer.

5. Mr. Curtis drove 649 miles one week and 234 miles the next week. How many miles did he drive in all?

- ○ 873
- ○ 875
- ● 883
- ○ 973

6. Mrs. Fox drove 168 miles one week and 518 miles the next week. How many miles did she drive in all?

- ○ 676
- ○ 678
- ● 686
- ○ 688

Name ______________________________

LESSON 29.3

Understand Plan Solve Check

Model 3-Digit Addition: Regroup Tens

Add.

1. Mrs. Dehmel read 252 pages in her book on Monday. She read 175 pages on Tuesday. How many pages did she read in the two days?

427 pages

2. There are 167 children in Grade 2. There are 165 children in Grade 1. How many children are there in the two grades together?

332 children

3. Mac watches two movies. The first is 134 minutes long. The second is 185 minutes long. How long are the two movies together?

319 minutes

4. Dorothy has 426 pennies in one jar. She has 186 pennies in another jar. How many pennies does she have in all?

612 pennies

Mark the correct answer.

5. Alex has 2 bags of marbles. There are 154 marbles in each bag. How many marbles does he have in all?

- ○ 154
- ○ 254
- ○ 208
- ● 308

6. Kristin has 2 sticker books. There are 155 stickers in one book. There are 125 stickers in the other book. How many stickers does she have in all?

- ○ 318
- ○ 308
- ● 280
- ○ 218

Name ____________________

Understand Plan Solve Check

Mental Math: Subtract Hundreds

Each bundle of paper contains 100 sheets. Solve.

1. April has 7 bundles of paper. She gives 4 to Joe. How many sheets of paper does April have left?

   __7__ hundreds − __4__ hundreds = __3__ hundreds

   __700__ − __400__ = __300__

2. Vincent has 4 bundles of paper. He gives 3 to Curt. How many sheets of paper does Vincent have left?

   __4__ hundreds − __3__ hundreds = __1__ hundred

   __400__ − __300__ = __100__

3. Farrah has 6 bundles of paper. She gives 2 to Jack. How many sheets of paper does Farrah have left?

   __6__ hundreds − __2__ hundreds = __4__ hundreds

   __600__ − __200__ = __400__

Mark the correct answer.

4. Which is the difference?
   800 − 600 = ?

   ○ 500
   ○ 400
   ○ 300
   ● 200

5. Which is the difference?
   5 hundreds − 2 hundreds = ?

   ○ 1 hundred
   ○ 2 hundreds
   ● 3 hundreds
   ○ 4 hundreds

Name ________________________________

LESSON 29.5

Understand Plan Solve Check

Model 3-Digit Subtraction: Regroup Tens

Use Workmat 5 and 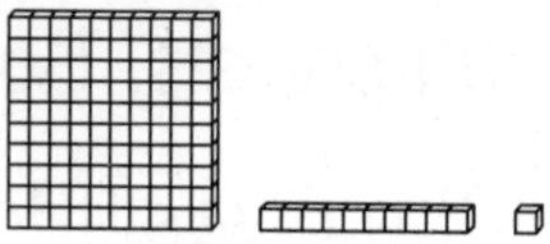.
Solve.

1. A grizzly bear weighs 582 pounds. A black bear weighs 355 pounds. How many more pounds does the grizzly bear weigh than the black bear?

   227 more pounds

2. The baby bear weighs 137 pounds. The mother bear weighs 346. How many more pounds does the mother bear weigh than the baby?

   209 pounds

3. A black bear weighs 369 pounds. A polar bear weighs 584 pounds. How many more pounds does the polar bear weigh than the black bear?

   215 pounds

4. The mother polar bear weighs 878 pounds. The baby polar bear weighs 365 pounds. How many more pounds does the mother weigh than the baby?

   513 more pounds

Mark the correct answer.

5. The second grade collected 542 cans of food. The first grade collected 214 cans. How many more cans did the second grade collect than the first grade?

   ● 328
   ○ 332
   ○ 358
   ○ 756

6. There are 984 children at East School. There are 738 children at West School. How many more children are there at East School than at West School?

   ○ 256
   ○ 254
   ● 246
   ○ 244